MW00720171

On The Street Where You Live

Pioneer Pathways of Early Victoria

For Peggy,

Enjoy!

Danda Humphreys

Danda Humphreys

Heritage House

CANADIAN CATALOGUING IN PUBLICATION DATA

Humphreys, Danda.
    On the street where you live

Includes index.
        ISBN 1-895811-90-2 (bound)
        ISBN 1-895811-98-8 (paperback)

        1. Street names—British Columbia—Victoria—History. 2. Victoria(B.C.)—History.
3. Victoria (B.C.)—Biography. I. Title.

FC3846.67.H85 1999   971.1'28   C99-910742-9
F1089.5.V6H85 1999

First bound edition 1999
First paperback edition 2001

Heritage House acknowledges the financial support for our publishing program from the Government of Canada through the Book Publishing Industry Development Program (BPIDP), Canada Council for the Arts, and the British Columbia Arts Council. The publisher would also like to thank Paul Bennett of the *Times Colonist*, Laurette Agnew of Saanich Pioneers' Society Archives, Ron Bradley and Daisy Bligh of Metchosin School Museum Society, Sister Margaret Cantwell of Sisters of St. Ann Archives, Geoffrcy Castle and Jack McIntyre of Saanich Archives, Carey Pallister of City of Victoria Archives, and Jack and Heather Waters of Bannockburn.

Front cover painting by Sarah Crease.
Back cover originally published in *Illustrated British Columbia* (1889) and hand-coloured by artist Michael Dean of Ladysmith, B.C.

Design and layout by Darlene Nickull
Maps by Brenda Martin
Edited by Audrey McClellan

HERITAGE HOUSE PUBLISHING COMPANY LTD.
#108 – 17665 66 A Avenue, Surrey, BC V3S 2A7

Printed in Canada

For Stanley and Molly Morris, who started me on the street called Life and would be tickled pink to see where it's taken me.

ACKNOWLEDGEMENTS

A book is never the work of the author alone, and *On the Street Where You Live* is no exception. Some very special people helped me along the way.

Times Colonist "Islander" editors Peter Salmon (first half of the book) and Paul Bennett (second half) were unwavering in their enthusiasm and support of the "Street" series.

It was Henry Gautier's "Why don't you write a book about street names?" that put me on the path to publication.

Thanks to Trevor Livelton and Carey Pallister of Victoria City Archives. Carey's energy, efficiency, and encouragement while helping me ferret out facts were invaluable. Thanks also to Geoffrey Castle and Jack McIntyre of Saanich Archives; Doug Nelson, Base Historian at CFB Esquimalt; the staff at the Provincial Archives of British Columbia and the Esquimalt Municipal Archives; Metchosin School Museum Society; Terry Malone at Sooke Region Museum; and all those wonderful volunteers at the Saanich Pioneer Society's Log Cabin.

People from all across Canada, parts of the U.S., the U.K., and New Zealand contacted me about their ancestors, then helped bring their stories to life by providing original written memorials, filling out details, lending photographs, and sharing tales handed down through the generations. For specific help with group and family histories, I am indebted to Sister Margaret Cantwell (Sisters of St. Ann),

Maureen Duffus (Yates family), Alan and Phyllis Duval (the Cheesemans), Dorothy Laundy (the Cridge family), Jan Ross, curator of Carr House, and Chris Hanna (the Carr family).

A big thank-you to John Adams, of the Old Cemeteries Society, who shared information, sneak-previewed each piece, and corrected my compass bearings. Thanks also to Fred Hook, for Ross Bay Cemetery burial records; Gayle Baird, for passenger list details; and Brad Morrison, for helpful comments.

A tip of the hat to Heritage House, who saw in this material the makings of a book, and particularly to my editor, Audrey McClellan, who waited in the wings till the last word was writ, then blew in like a breath of fresh air to clean me up and turn the series into a book.

Here's to the authors, journalists, and historians who over the years have captured the essence of our city in their respective articles, books, and journals (see the Bibliography).

Here's to the diarists and writers of those far-off days, and to those who had the foresight to preserve their scribblings for posterity by donating them to the various public archives.

And last but not least, here's to all the "Islander" readers—too numerous to mention, but you know who you are!—whose ideas, comments, and constant encouragement have turned a peek at our pioneering past into a fascinating and exhilarating journey. This book is for you.

Victoria and Outlying Areas

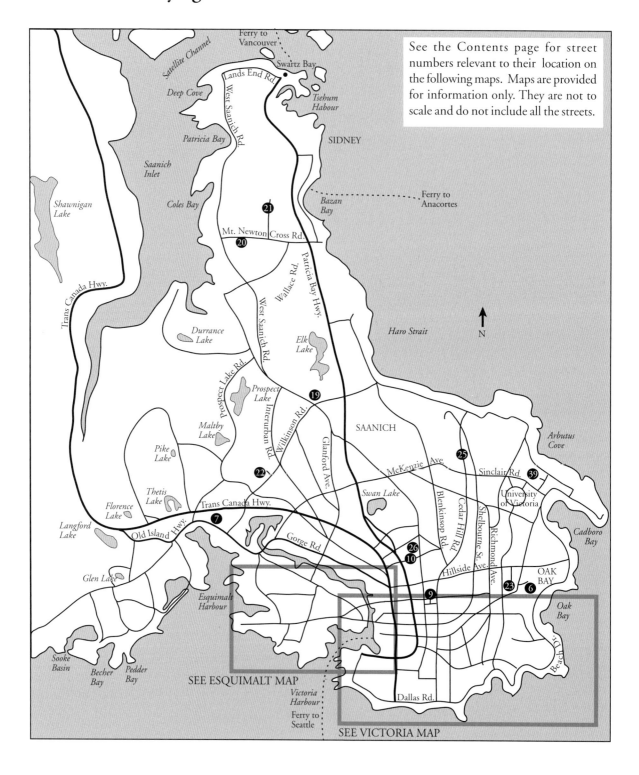

See the Contents page for street numbers relevant to their location on the following maps. Maps are provided for information only. They are not to scale and do not include all the streets.

Victoria and Oak Bay

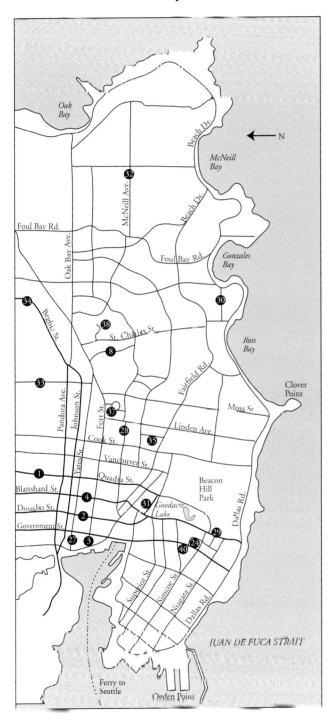

Esquimalt

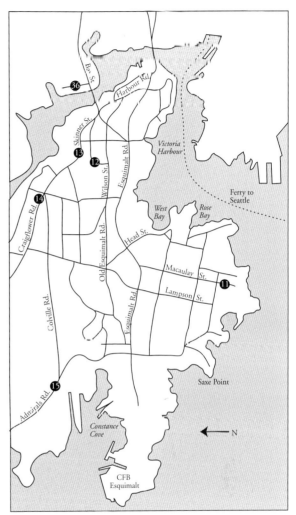

Sooke and Metchosin

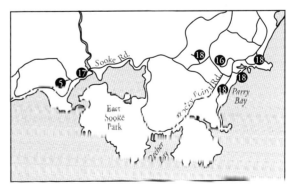

This 1848 drawing by P.M. O'Leary shows the recently completed Fort Victoria. The Hudson's Bay Company flag dominated the skyline, and the HBC dominated the political, economic, and social life of the town, especially after Chief Factor James Douglas was appointed colonial governor in 1851. Below, Newton Brett's "The Founding of Victoria, 1843," was commissioned in 1943 to adorn a centennial calendar.

INTRODUCTION

Have you ever thought much about the name of the street where you live? Street names have always fascinated me. Most Canadian cities have Broadways and Mains and Kings and Queens and Fronts, and there may be an interesting story behind them all. However, it's the more unusual names that tweak my curiosity. When I look up at street signs I wonder, "Who are these people? What brought them here? Why is this street named after them?"

Like so many other cities, Victoria tells its history through its street names. Many Victoria streets are named after individuals from the early pioneering days. These streets—Douglas, Finlayson, Tolmie, to name but a few—remind us that those first residents of Victoria were not simply the usual handful of hardy pioneers. They were employees of the Hudson's Bay Company (HBC).

The HBC had been operating in Canada since the 1600s. In the 1700s the Company opened up the West, and by the 1800s it was firmly established in several small posts and one larger one—Fort Vancouver, on the Columbia River in the Oregon country. But in the 1840s, as American settlers poured into the area, which had been held jointly by Britain and the United States, it became clear that Britain and the HBC would soon lose control of this territory. When talk of a border between British and American territory made it clear the boundary would be far north of Fort Vancouver, the HBC superintendent sent James Douglas up the coast to search for a suitable site for a new fort. Douglas found a spot on the southern tip of Vancouver Island. The Songhee nation that inhabited the area called it Camossung. Douglas renamed it for the young British queen.

Fort Victoria was strategically located on the east side of the Inner Harbour. It was like a little town unto itself, with its barracks, office buildings, and company store protected by nine-pounder cannons and an eighteen-foot-high palisade. A trail leading from the east gate of the fort quickly disappeared into the forest, en route to the Native village at Cadboro Bay.

In 1846 the Oregon Treaty did indeed establish a border between the United States and the British colonies west of the Rockies. Following the 49th parallel from east to west, the border took a dogleg south at the coastline and left Vancouver Island to the British. Douglas and his superiors heaved sighs of relief.

The little settlement slowly spread beyond the palisades. Farms provided food and dairy products for the fort. A dozen or so houses dotted the landscape. Trails connected the fort with the Company farms and with the few brave pioneers who had settled farther afield.

The first James Bay Bridge, built in 1859 and shown above in the 1860s, connected Government Street to the site of the new legislature. Affectionately referred to as "The Birdcages," the five main colonial administration buildings (below) were completed between 1858 and 1862. They were home to B.C.'s politicians and bureaucrats until the end of the nineteenth century.

In 1849 the British government leased Vancouver Island to the HBC for an annual payment of seven shillings—about $3. In return, the Company agreed to actively promote significant British settlement. Two years passed without evidence of any such settlement. The British started agitating for action. Douglas, by this time governor of the colony and anxious to keep his part of the bargain, hired a surveyor to create streets, divide the land, and generally make sense of the jumble that surrounded the fort.

J.D. Pemberton's mandate was to prepare a town plan and a general structure for colonization that would discourage squatters, paupers, and land speculators. His plan comprised town lots, suburban lots, and country lots. Business-people and merchants would work in the town and live in the suburbs; farmers would occupy the outer areas. It was, in short, a structure that closely mirrored the traditional class divisions of England.

Between 1852 and 1855, Pemberton and his assistant mapped out the land surrounding the fort. Four streets traced its perimeters. Government Street—officially the first street in British North America west of the Rockies—acknowledged the presence of the first government offices near the corner of what is now Yates Street. The street ended at the water's edge, south of the fort, where the tide flowed briefly inland, forming what would later be called James's Bay. Fort Street was the official name given to the now-widened trail leading from the fort's east gate. Wharf Street ran along the wharf west of the fort. The fourth street, next to a ravine that divided the fort from the land north of it, was named Johnson; a century later, nobody could remember why.

Douglas's census of 1854 recorded a total of 232 residents in the town. Almost half were under the age of twenty. There were 79 houses, while twelve stores and shops catered to the populace's needs.

By 1858 there were a few more dwellings and a few more people—about 300 all told. But in April of that year the unexpected arrival of hordes of people headed for the Fraser River gold fields pulled the little town out of the past and into a potentially profitable future. The population doubled when the first boatload of miners stepped ashore. Hotels, trading posts, and saloons sprang up on every corner. Business was booming. There was only one problem: none of Victoria's new inhabitants could find their way around.

Clearly something had to be done, and on September 16, 1858, the *Victoria Gazette* trumpeted the arrival of the town's "new baby"—an official street map. Street names had been selected by the colonial surveyor, reported the newspaper, and the map was available for viewing by all and sundry at the Land Office.

In his wisdom, Pemberton had selected names according to several distinct classifications. Governors and explorers were honoured first. Juan Francisco de la Bodega y Quadra is acknowledged in this category, as are Richard Blanshard and James Douglas. Surprisingly—or not surprisingly, given Douglas's stature—his street was the one that ran smack bang through the middle of town. Vancouver Street, commemorating the man for whom the island was named long before Douglas spied it, was pushed three blocks to the east. Along with George Vancouver, navigator James Cook was similarly honoured.

Not all streets were named after people. Constance, Pandora, Cormorant, Fisgard,

By 1878, twenty years after the first invasion of gold seekers, Victoria had taken on a decidedly urban character. In the foreground, the James Bay area was well established. Note that the harbour extends under a bridge between James Bay and downtown. This area, the James Bay mudflats, was eventually reclaimed and became the site of the Empress Hotel, the Crystal Gardens, and an extension of Douglas Street.

Discovery, Herald, Chatham, and Pembroke recorded the names of ships that had visited the area. North American cities, rivers, and lakes were remembered in streets such as Montreal, Quebec, Toronto, St. Lawrence, Michigan, Erie, Huron, Superior, and Ontario.

The map made official the names that had arisen out of common usage. A street might be named for its inhabitants or for its dimensions. Kanaka Road or Row (now Humboldt Street) was so called because a number of Hawaiians lived in cabins there. Some street names were decidedly tongue-in-cheek. For a short time Broad Street, named by some wag for its narrowness, took on the grander name of Broadway, but soon reverted to its former status.

And nowhere else in North America could you find a View Street without a view.

At one point, as was the custom in many towns on this continent, some streets were given a number instead of a name. To the east of Victoria's Inner Harbour, nine streets ran from north to south. That was the extent of the town; east of the ninth street was dense forest, swampland, and rocks. The northern ends of those north-south streets were first numbered and later renamed, thus: First (Douglas), Second (Rose, now Blanshard), Third (Wark), Fourth (Quadra), Fifth (Fifth), Sixth (Vancouver), Seventh (Graham), Eighth (Prior), Ninth (Blackwood). Fifth Street is the odd one out— for some unknown reason it was never renamed. No one knows who Rose might have been, but we do know that John Work, a long-time HBC man and the owner of Hillside Farm, had sons-in-law whose last names were Graham, Prior, and Blackwood.

Disillusioned by their working and living conditions, many of the men brought out to work for the HBC or on the HBC Puget's Sound Agricultural Company farms quickly moved away from the area surrounding the fort. A few were independent settlers; most were indentured servants, with the option to purchase an acreage at the end of their five-year contract. Most of the latter group put as much distance as possible between themselves and their former employers, striking out on their own for other parts of the peninsula.

That wasn't as simple as it seemed. The journey from the Inner Harbour to Mount Newton, for example, often took four or five days along winding Indian trails. The Native people followed the animals, and animals don't move in straight lines from A to B—they follow the easiest route.

The alternative was to travel by canoe around the coastline. This was the only option for those who settled in places like Sooke or Metchosin. The first settlers arrived there in the late 1840s, and it would be many years before a road was built out to these Western Communities. Captain W.C. Grant regularly travelled to and from Sooke by canoe. When Martha Cheney married Henry Ella at Bilston Farm in Metchosin, guests rode on horseback in their wedding finery to take part in the celebrations. Dr. J.S. Helmcken made house calls on horseback. Before churches were built, the Anglican dean, Edward Cridge, rode out to Esquimalt, Colwood, Sooke, Metchosin, Royal Oak, Mount Newton, and Nanaimo,

baptizing, marrying, and burying as he went. Eventually the horse trails were widened to allow horse-drawn wagons and carriages to pass. Later still they were widened even more, to accommodate the to-and-fro flow of automobiles and delivery vehicles.

Streets were named willy-nilly, and around the end of the nineteenth century it became evident that duplication of street names was causing confusion. City council drafted a by-law to change the relevant names and instituted a new system for street numbering. Dallas Road became the starting point for the numbering of all streets running north. Streets running east were numbered from an imaginary line extending north from the outer wharf to Harriet Road. A decimal system was used. An even hundred was allotted to each block, with a new number every twenty feet. The south and east sides of streets bore odd numbers; north and west sides, even numbers.

Street names changed over the years, mostly at the whim of the city fathers, and there are few records to show when and why the various changes were made. Some streets are named for the people who once owned the land. The lane leading to a farmhouse or other dwelling might be named for its chief occupant, such as Tod Road in Oak Bay. Other times the street takes the name of the dwelling itself, as in Pentrelew Place off Fort Street, Marifield Avenue in James Bay, or Bilston Place in Metchosin. The origins of street names in outlying areas are easier to pinpoint, as they almost always reflect the men who settled there.

We have streets named after poets such as Kipling, Byron, and Tennyson (no Shakespeare – our Shakespeare Street is named after HBC contractor Noah Shakespeare). The Marigold area,

This rendering of the site of today's Bastion Square shows one of the fort's bastions in 1862, two years before the fort was completely dismantled.

with street names like Lily, Jasmine, Violet, Tulip, Iris, and Gardenia, sounds like an English country garden. HBC and other farms are remembered in streets such as Hillside, Cloverdale, Fairfield, Fernwood, Towner, Downey, and Mills. Wellington, Waterloo, and Howe streets recall famous battles and statesmen. Many of the early street names commemorating women have disappeared over the decades. The ones that remain include Joan (Dunsmuir) Crescent, Harriet (Yates) Road, and Josette (Work) Place.

To this day, Victoria has the very English habit of calling one street two or more different names. Thus we have Richardson-McNeill—all the same street. Likewise, Fairfield Road-Beach Drive; Foul Bay-Henderson-University Drive; and the best one of all, Dallas Road—with several name changes before it finally peters out at the north end of Cordova Bay.

At the south end of the peninsula, numerous doglegged streets remind us that when large estates were eventually subdivided—all at different times—the streets in one subdivision somehow never matched the streets in another. Joseph Pemberton would not have been amused.

There have been some interesting "hiccups" along the way, as mapmakers' errors became the accepted spelling. (Lansing O.) Swart's Bay

"Entrance to the Harbour of Victoria. The harbour of the city proper offers accommodation only for vessels drawing eighteen feet of water and under, but improvements are continually being made and the adjacent and supplementary harbour of Esquimalt supplies all that may be lacking here. A fine macadamized road connects the two ports, along which is stretched a telephone line."
(*Drawing and caption from* Illustrated British Columbia, *1884*)

became Swartz Bay; Prince's Street (to go with King's and Queen's) became Princess; Huggins (for a Work son-in-law, Edward Huggins) became Higgins, and so on.

But always our street names bring us back to the early times, when those first pioneers braved the journey from their homeland. They reflect and honour the men, women, and children who came here when the only names in existence were those given by the first residents of this land. Many areas—Sooke, Metchosin, Saanich, Songhees—still bear the names bestowed on them by First Nations people.

There are probably more than 3000 streets in Victoria and its outlying areas. Each street name tells a story, some of them intensely personal, all of them fascinating. This book affords a snapshot glimpse of just a few of the people who lived here during Victoria's first quarter century.

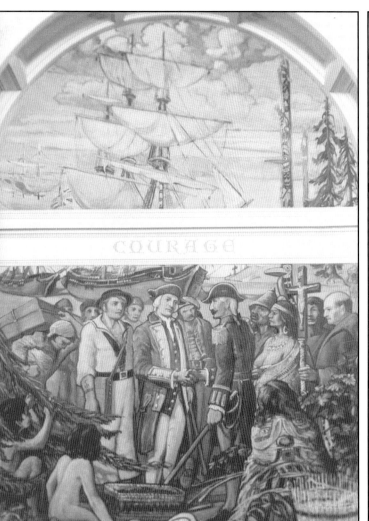

Captain Quadra visited the B.C. coast in the late 1700s and was the Spanish commandant at Nootka when Captain George Vancouver arrived in 1792 to take formal possession of the lands under terms of a British-Spanish agreement known as the Nootka Convention. A mural (left) in the B.C. Parliament Buildings depicts this event. Less well known is the stained glass panel (right), a 1957 gift from the Spanish government, which shows the August 28, 1792, meeting of Quadra and Vancouver. It is now housed in the missionary Father Brabant's original church at Friendly Cove on Nootka Sound. The ships in the background are Quadra's Active *and HMS* Discovery.

Victoria's Spanish connection

From its beginnings at Beacon Hill Park to its abrupt end at Glanford Avenue and West Saanich Road, Quadra is a street of contrasts.

It starts by pushing along the edge of Victoria's busy downtown core, its cathedral, red brick churches, and school gradually giving way to apartment buildings and plazas. Along its lazy northward curves, taller houses stretch up to find a view over the roofs of neat ranchers. Condominiums and professional buildings jostle for space on either side of its undulating surface.

Rounding the gentle bend at Rock Street, Mount Douglas looms ahead. Then it's across McKenzie and past bigger, grander homes until another gentle bend reveals a sweeping view northward. A little farther along, Quadra passes over the Pat Bay Highway only to disappear as suddenly as it started at its junction with West Saanich and Glanford.

A very fine street indeed, a fitting reminder of a time over 200 years ago and of the man the street was named for.

Don Juan Francisco de la Bodega y Quadra was one of many adventurers who sailed to the Northwest Coast in the latter part of the eighteenth century. In those early days, Russian and British explorers vied with the Spanish in their eagerness to claim portions of the "new land" for their respective countries.

Quadra was a Creole naval officer from Peru who arrived on this coast aboard the *Sonora* in 1776, the same year the original thirteen renegade colonies on the east coast of the continent achieved independence. Barely big enough to hold Quadra, the hydrographic surveyor who accompanied him, and a fourteen-man crew, this small schooner made slow and difficult headway.

It can't have been a comfortable voyage, with cramped quarters, scurvy, and not even enough room below decks to stand upright. Yet the men were in high spirits. After battling their way through heavy seas, they anchored near Mount Fairweather and took formal possession of the land for Spain before heading for home.

In 1792 Quadra sailed here again, this time to meet Captain George Vancouver, who along with Lieutenant-Commander William Broughton was conducting his own expedition to the Northwest Coast. Quadra was 49 years old. Vancouver was in his mid-30s.

The two hit it off immediately. Despite their inability to speak each other's language, there was mutual respect and enjoyment of each other's company. They settled on a name that

From 1855 until 1872, the Quadra Street Burying Ground was Victoria's cemetery (above). In the early years of the twentieth century it was converted into a park. The grave markers were removed, though some monuments were left in place and several markers were grouped at the eastern end of the grassy lawn (below). Now it is known as Pioneer Square, and the Old Cemeteries Society conducts evening lantern tours there in the summer, recounting stories of early Victoria.

recognized the rapport between Spaniard and Briton—Quadra's and Vancouver's Island. Today we know it simply as Vancouver Island.

∽ ∽ ∽ ∽

Less than a century after Quadra left these shores, the sleepy Hudson's Bay Company outpost called Fort Victoria was rudely awakened by an invasion of rowdy gold miners en route to the Fraser River.

By late 1858 the influx of settlers and of sicknesses such as smallpox had rendered the burying ground at the HBC fort woefully inadequate. Not only was it too small, it was also troubled by vandals and by cattle and swine that insisted on rooting around in the mud and digging up the corpses. In 1855 the Quadra Street Cemetery had been opened at Quadra and Rockland, and in 1859 a Bastion Square Prison chain gang helped move the remaining bodies from the fort to their new resting place.

In those days, Quadra Street was on the outskirts of town. Surprisingly, although the cemetery was on relatively high ground, it was swampy and impossible to drain. Gun carriages bearing the coffins of naval officers would become stuck in the mud as the horses pulling them struggled up the Quadra Street hill. At the burying site, the ground was so wet that often a man would have to stand on the coffin until there was enough earth shovelled in to weigh it down in its water-filled grave.

Before long, this burying ground was also full. Ross Bay Cemetery was established, and by 1882 the Quadra Street burying ground had fallen prey to vandals, cattle, and swine, like the fort burying ground before it. It was eventually cleared of most of its markers and turned into a park—but not before it had become the final resting place for many of Victoria's pioneers. They rest there to this day, many in unmarked graves, their stories recounted each summer during public tours of what we now know as Pioneer Square.

Juan Francisco de la Bodega y Quadra is remembered in Victoria by the street that bears his name. Once it was a muddy track bordering a young town; today it's a major artery running through the heart of a busy city.

Canada begins on Douglas

*T*oday, Douglas Street cuts a northward swath from the southwest corner of Beacon Hill Park at Dallas Road. It's an important street, running through the heart of our city, taking us from the shores of the Strait of Juan de Fuca to the start of a cross-continental journey on the Trans-Canada Highway. It is a fitting reminder of the man who, almost 160 years ago, took the first step toward putting Victoria on the North American map.

The year was 1842. The place: Fort Vancouver on the Columbia River, which since 1827 had been the Hudson's Bay Company's western headquarters. By the early 1840s it had become clear to HBC Governor George Simpson and General Superintendent Dr. John McLoughlin that the proposed boundary between British and American territory was to be farther north than anticipated, and Fort Vancouver would shortly be on the wrong side of it. McLoughlin gave his assistant, James Douglas, an assignment—to set sail for the southern end of Vancouver Island and decide on a suitable site for a new fort.

Rejecting Sooke and Esquimalt harbours as unsuitable, Douglas chose the "Port of Camosack" (his version of the Songhees' "Camossung," encompassing today's Inner Harbour), which he said was safe and accessible, with fine timber, suitable for construction, growing nearby. There was also a canal with a tidal force capable of driving the most powerful machinery.

The Port of Camosack was renamed for the British queen of the day. Camosack is now spelled Camosun. The "canal of Camosack" is now known as The Gorge. And James Douglas has taken his rightful place in Victoria's—and British Columbia's—history.

Who was this man? What brought him to these parts? What forces shaped his life and determined that he should be remembered by those of us who now live in the place he once described as "the perfect 'Eden' in the midst of the dreary wilderness of the northwest coast"?

James and Amelia Douglas

The governor's mansion was built on the south shore of James Bay in 1851. Eight years later the new colonial administration buildings were constructed next door. Douglas's house was torn down in 1906, but a cairn behind the Royal British Columbia Museum marks the spot where it stood.

James Douglas was born in 1803 in Guyana (formerly British Guiana) to the Creole mistress of a Scottish merchant. He was one of three children of this union. His parents never married—in fact, John Douglas later married another woman—but his father took his responsibilities seriously, arranging education for his sons in Scotland.

At sixteen, his schooling completed and wanderlust upon him, young James set sail from Liverpool, England, bound for Montreal and a career in the fur trade. He journeyed west, crossing the Rockies and arriving in Fort McLeod in what was then known as New Caledonia. It was at his next post, Fort St. James, that he met the woman who would share his life.

Amelia Connolly was the sixteen-year-old daughter of Chief Factor William Connolly. She too was of mixed blood, the daughter of an Irish-Canadian man and a Cree woman. As a child, Amelia had moved around a great deal with her family—to various posts in northern Manitoba, to Cumberland House in Saskatchewan, Lesser Slave Lake in Alberta, and Fort St. James in northern B.C. Each time the family moved it meant a long canoe journey with many portages along the way. Amelia had had a hard life, with frequent shortages of food, violence among rival fur traders, and an inhospitable climate.

The HBC encouraged its fur traders to marry Native or Metis women. The Company felt that a Native escort afforded protection for its men—assuming that Native people would be less likely to attack one of their own. In 1828 Amelia and James were joined, as Amelia's parents had been, in a form of marriage known as "the custom of the country." Their marriage was not solemnized by a clergyman until almost a decade later, but it was by all accounts a happy union and a mutually supportive one.

There are many stories about Amelia. One of the most famous concerns an altercation between James and the Carrier Indians at Fort St. James. James had tracked down an alleged murderer and had him executed in the Carrier village near the fort. Chief Kwah took offence at this and arrived at the fort ready for revenge. Kwah's nephew overcame James and held a knife at his throat, waiting for the signal to end his life.

Amelia, who had apparently heard the commotion and sensed the danger her husband was in, quickly gathered blankets and other items of value to the Carrier, and threw them down in front of the warriors as an offering.

The ploy worked. The Carrier accepted the gifts and left the fort without harming James. Had it not been for Amelia's quick action, her husband would surely have been killed and Victoria's history might have been very different.

Amelia gave birth to thirteen children over the next 25 years, though only six survived infancy. The first, also called Amelia, was born in the fall of 1829, just before James was transferred to Fort Vancouver. The child died when she was just a few months old. In the spring, Amelia followed her husband to Fort Vancouver. Ten children were born there, and after the family moved to Fort Victoria in 1849, two more children arrived.

In 1851 the Douglases built a home overlooking James Bay, where the Royal British Columbia Museum stands today. It was a grand, two-storey affair, with dormer windows facing north across the harbour toward the fort and gardens that ran down to the water. The family could easily reach the fort by following a path along the south side of James Bay to where a wooden plank crossed the small stream at the bay's blind end.

In 1852 Douglas purchased 500 acres of HBC land east of his home. His estate, Fairfield, bounded by Fort Street to the north and the Strait of Juan de Fuca to the south, encompassed most of the present-day Fairfield and Rockland areas.

Perhaps because of their own uncertain childhoods, James and Amelia held strongly to the tradition of family life. They were typical Victorian parents. James tended toward strictness. Amelia was overprotective. Both doted on their offspring. An impressive,

After the 1858 gold rush, interest in the remote colony of Vancouver Island grew in England. On January 18, 1863, The Illustrated London News *published this engraving. Distinguishable landmarks include Victoria District Church on the hilltop, the paddlewheeler SS* Beaver *in the harbour, James Bay Bridge leading toward Governor Douglas's residence, and Douglas's 500-acre Fairfield estate in the background. Farther right are the government buildings known as "The Birdcages."*

autocratic man to his colleagues, James was a stern but fond husband and father, writing long letters to England when his children were in school there, and treating their mother with the utmost care and respect.

While James became ever more prominent, serving as governor of the colonies of Vancouver Island and British Columbia, Amelia lived a simpler and somewhat lonelier life. She was shunned by the English society ladies who arrived in Victoria during the 1850s and 1860s, presumably because of her illegitimate status. Undeterred, she focused on her children and her chickens.

When James was knighted by Queen Victoria in 1864, Lady Amelia Douglas stood proudly beside him. But it wasn't until 1869, when her parents' marriage was officially recognized, that she felt able to take her rightful place in society.

Sir James Douglas died in 1877. Amelia outlived him by thirteen years, remaining until her own death in 1890 in the house they had shared, near the street that still bears their name. They are buried together in Ross Bay Cemetery.

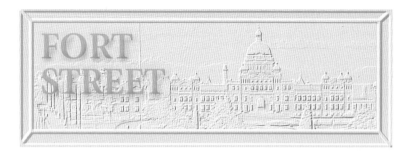

Gateway from history

Watching the crowds throng the junction of Fort and Wharf streets today, it's hard to imagine how it must have looked when James Douglas first saw the area in 1842.

Today the restaurants, coffee shops, and antique and art emporiums along Fort Street's flat western reaches give way to a gentle hill at Moss Street. A left-hand bend at St. Charles takes the road to the Oak Bay Junction and across Richmond, where lazy curves lead to the intersection with Foul Bay and the street's present-day continuation as Cadboro Bay Road. Over 150 years ago it was a simple trail leading east from the harbour of Camosack.

After James Douglas reported to the authorities at Fort Vancouver that Camosack was a good spot for a fort, he returned a year later to choose the actual building site. The *Beaver*, with Douglas and his men aboard, steamed into what is now the Inner Harbour. In an open glade on the harbour's eastern shore, where a steep fall-off of the rocky shoreline made it possible for deep-sea vessels to tie up alongside, they decided to build their fort.

Finding many oak trees but few cedars to supply picketing, Douglas was quick to approach the Songhees people for help. The Songhees understood the concept of forts; their own, at Cadboro Bay, had always protected them well against raiding foes. They agreed to accept one blanket for every 40 pickets they provided, and Douglas lent them three large axes to help them in their work.

Designed to be the HBC's main depot on the Pacific coast, Fort Victoria was an impressive sight. Comprising a 300-by-300-foot quadrangle surrounded by an 18-foot stockade, it contained administrative buildings and accommodations as well as outhouses, workshops, and a company store constructed of Western fir or red cedar logs. Cedar shakes covered the rafters. Octagonal bastions equipped with nine-pound cannons fortified the stockade. On the east and west sides of the stockade were two large gates. The gate on the east side led to the road that was named Fort Street.

At first the Natives were cautious. Then, encouraged by their positive relationship with Douglas, Charles Ross, Roderick Finlayson (the latter two left in charge of the fort when Douglas returned to his job at Fort Vancouver), and the HBC men, they moved closer. Eventually they moved their camp to the Inner Harbour's western shore, opposite the fort, and helped clear the land around it for farms.

This 1860 Sarah Crease sketch shows the inside of Fort Victoria shortly before it was dismantled. The western gate of the fort, pictured centre, led out onto the wharf. The pathway across the compound led to the eastern gate, and from there became Fort Street, which continued on to Cadboro Bay.

Gradually buildings went up around the fort as HBC retirees and other colonists arrived. During the next few years, fur trading and trapping gave way to farming, salmon-curing, and lumbering, activities that supplied the Royal Navy ships which had arrived to protect the British subjects. American whaling ships, Russian ships, and trading posts enjoyed a flourishing trade with the HBC and independent traders.

In 1846 the boundary was established between the United States and British North America, and plans were made to abandon Fort Vancouver. Fort Victoria was enlarged and assumed the role of HBC Pacific headquarters,

and in 1849 the British Crown leased Vancouver Island to the Hudson's Bay Company for seven shillings a year—on the condition that the HBC promoted settlement in the area. That was also the year James Douglas returned to Fort Victoria as chief factor, the trader-in-charge. He lived with his family inside the fort enclosure until their own residence was built in 1851.

Fort Victoria was slow to grow...until the spring of 1858, when the outpost of a few hundred people swelled to nearly 30,000 with the arrival of people in search of the Fraser River's gold. The miners lived in tents, looking to the fort's storehouse for supplies, until they set sail for the Mainland. Returning a few months later

Fort Street has always played a prominent if sometimes controversial role in Victoria's history. In 1876 Lord Dufferin, representing the Canadian government, visited Victoria amid controversy over the transcontinental Canadian railway. The Canadian senate would only approve railway contracts through to Bute Inlet, ignoring previous commitments made in negotiations held at Carnarvon to continue the rails to Victoria. While the Fort Street arch, erected for Lord Dufferin's visit, appeared friendly from the eastern perspective, the motto inside the arch offered a more ominous ultimatum. Canadian Illustrated News *reported that Lord Dufferin was steered clear of this arch. The newspaper also commented that for B.C., "Isolated as they are, it [the railway] is a matter of life and death for them. And it really is so to the autonomy of the Dominion, and its maintaining a separate existence on the continent."*

Frederick Dally, one of the frontier's most capable photographers, stood on the southeast corner of Government Street to capture the north side of Fort Street heading east in the early 1860s. On the left is where the Eaton's Centre stands today.

carrying gold, they found that prices had risen in their absence. The town surrounding the fort had grown as other men and women arrived, hoping to profit from the gold miners' good fortune. There were houses, a jail, a hospital, and a fire hall. Gas-lit streets, drains, piped water, parks, paved roads, and sidewalks gradually made Victoria a more civilized place to live.

By 1860 the HBC's hold over this area had diminished, and in December 1860, when the gold rush was still filling the town with men and money, it was announced that the pickets surrounding the old fort and the bastion at the corner of View and Government streets were to be removed. The fort was no longer needed for government or commerce—birdcage-like legislative buildings had been built on the south side of James Bay, and stores were springing up everywhere. Victorians wanted to improve their environment and to have some control over local development, and the HBC land was needed for that development. The colonial legislature was pressured into passing an act that incorporated Victoria as a city in August 1862. A few weeks later, Victorians held their first council meeting at the police barracks that replaced the old fort.

Today the only evidence that the fort ever existed is the mooring rings that are still embedded in the rocks below Wharf Street's little park. Today Fort Street is a mecca for antique seekers and cappuccino lovers. Yesterday it was where Victoria began.

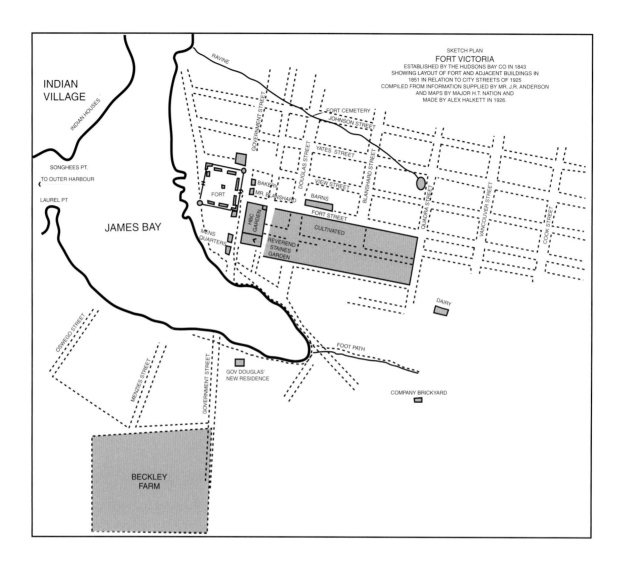

SKETCH PLAN
FORT VICTORIA
ESTABLISHED BY THE HUDSONS BAY CO IN 1843
SHOWING LAYOUT OF FORT AND ADJACENT BUILDINGS IN
1851 IN RELATION TO CITY STREETS OF 1925
COMPILED FROM INFORMATION SUPPLIED BY MR. J.R. ANDERSON
AND MAPS BY MAJOR H.T. NATION AND
MADE BY ALEX HALKETT IN 1926.

INDIAN VILLAGE

INDIAN HOUSES

SONGHEES PT.

TO OUTER HARBOUR

LAUREL PT

JAMES BAY

RAVINE

GOVERNMENT STREET

FORT CEMETERY

JOHNSON STREET

YATES STREET

DOUGLAS STREET

VIEW STREET

BLANSHARD STREET

QUADRA STREET

VANCOUVER STREET

COOK STREET

BAKERY

MR. BLANSHARD

BARNS

FORT STREET

FORT

HBC GARDEN

CULTIVATED

MENS QUARTERS

REVEREND STAINES GARDEN

DAIRY

OSWEGO STREET

MENZIES STREET

GOVERNMENT STREET

FOOT PATH

GOV DOUGLAS' NEW RESIDENCE

COMPANY BRICKYARD

BECKLEY FARM

*This sketch plan shows Fort Victoria in 1851, with an overlay of the city's streets from 1925.
At the time of his resignation, a disenchanted Governor Blanshard resided outside the fort
gate at the corner of Government Street, while James Douglas also lived outside the walls,
near the northeast bastion, awaiting completion of his new residence across James Bay.*

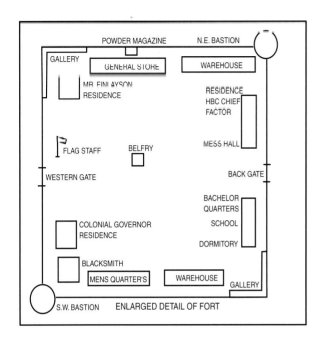

These sketches, made by Alec Halbett from photographs by Richard Maynard, show the layout of Fort Victoria before it was razed. Above, the square fort featured bastions on its southwest and northeast corners to provide protection to all four sides. The western gate close to the flag staff faced the harbour. The eastern gate opened onto today's Government Street, with the two buildings depicted below on either side of the gate. The belfry stands before the HBC chief factor's residence, which included quarters for junior clerks and a mess hall. Right of the gate, the two-level structure included bachelor quarters, a schoolroom, both a doctor's and chaplain's quarters, and an upper dormitory.

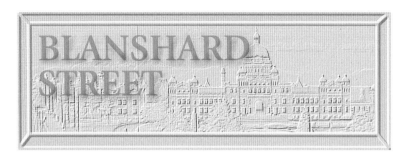

The first governor

*I*f ever there was a street that mimicked a man's experience, it's Blanshard. This street comes up out of nowhere, appearing as a continuation of Belleville before becoming bold enough to drive northward on a course of sweeping curves and rolling hills.

Its life in the city is short, just as Blanshard's was. For most of its length Blanshard parallels Douglas, and indeed the two were destined to go down in history side by side. But where Douglas Street takes flight and soars majestically on as the beginning of the road that crosses Canada, Blanshard Street rounds a curve and disappears into oblivion as a road with another name. Oblivion was also the plight of Richard Blanshard.

One can only guess at Blanshard's thoughts as the HMS *Driver* left Panama in 1850 and made its way up the coast to Fort Victoria. At 32, with an Oxford education and some years of legal experience behind him, Blanshard was honoured to have been appointed the first

HMS Driver *(left), which brought Vancouver Island's first governor (above), was portrayed by Sir Oswald Walters Brierly in 1854. The two-master was one of the Royal Navy vessels that made Esquimalt its home port in an era when the British Empire was still a force to be reckoned with.*

governor of Vancouver Island. It was a huge stepping-stone in the young barrister's career. After months of uncomfortable sea travel, he must have looked forward to reaching Victoria, establishing himself at Government House, and meeting the challenge of governing a new colony.

He was somewhat naive. He was probably misinformed. And without a doubt, he was in for a rude awakening.

On a cold March day, under leaden skies and with a foot of snow on the ground, the colony's first Royal Governor stepped ashore to an even colder reception. No preparations had been made for his arrival. There was no welcoming committee. Blanshard himself had to muster an unwilling group of British men and naval personnel at the fort as audience for his own reading of the proclamation that instituted British government in the Pacific Northwest. A few guns fired a desultory salute, and then the men dispersed and went back to work. The whole ceremony took less than an hour. Blanshard must have had the distinct impression that his first day on the job had not been a resounding success.

We don't know whether Blanshard was aware beforehand that news of his appointment had been poorly received by the fort's chief factor, who had wanted—expected—to be appointed to the post himself. Douglas was, after all, the founder of Fort Victoria and convinced that he knew better than anyone else how to develop the colony. But the British government had other ideas. Not wanting to give total control of the new colony to an HBC man, they had appointed a governor of their own.

Douglas was not pleased and showed his disapproval in a rather ungentlemanly fashion.

It wasn't so much what he did as what he *didn't* do. When Blanshard arrived, the promised residence wasn't ready. In fact it wasn't even started. Somehow or other, according to Douglas, the labourers had always been needed more urgently elsewhere.

With nowhere else to go, Blanshard had to return to the ship that had brought him. Shortly afterward, with provisions at the fort running low and a shipload of immigrants from England expected any time, the *Driver* was pressed into supply ship duty and set sail for Fort Nisqually in Puget's Sound, Washington Territory. Blanshard, having no other home, was forced to tag along, sharing the return journey with 86 cattle and 830 sheep. After about a month, a room was found for him at the fort.

From the outset it was made clear to Blanshard that he was an outsider. Practically everyone else at the fort was or had been allied to the Hudson's Bay Company—some for the best part of a lifetime. Blanshard didn't belong. With his university education and gentlemanly air, the barrister was out of his element in the rough-and-ready world of a Company outpost.

Blanshard was an interesting figure of a man. Doleful and soulful by nature, he found little at Fort Victoria to cheer him. Douglas ignored him, indeed he carried on as if the governor was not there. Company officers, impressed with Blanshard's quiet, unassuming manner but obliged to be loyal to their chief, followed suit. Only some independent settlers and the older schoolgirls, who thought the tall, elegant English lawyer with the military moustache and melancholy air a rather romantic figure, looked upon Blanshard as a welcome addition to the settlement.

Try as he might, Blanshard found himself in an impossible situation. All of his suggestions

The corner of Blanshard and Johnson streets was once home to stables and wagon yards.

were either unwelcome or totally ignored by the more powerful Douglas. The thousand acres of land he had been promised, which was supposed to provide him with rental income in lieu of a salary, was still barren—Douglas could never spare the farm labourers needed to develop it. Unlike the HBC men, Blanshard was offered no concessions and soon found the huge mark-up at the fort's supply store prohibitive.

When it was finally finished, six months after Blanshard's arrival, Government House—an 800-square-foot dwelling at Yates and Government—seemed like a barely concealed insult. With only four rooms, an attached kitchen, and a smaller house for his servants, the new governor would hardly be living in grand style.

It was the last straw. Seven months and one week after his arrival, Blanshard sent in his resignation to the Colonial Office. It would be ten months before he received word that it had been accepted. In the meantime, he found himself called to Fort Rupert to settle a dispute.

Some months earlier, Blanshard, perceiving Fort Rupert's Dr. Helmcken to be a fair, just, and capable man, had made him a magistrate and charged him with settling the troubles that had erupted at the northern fort. It was a disastrous move for all involved. Helmcken, unable to find and appoint special constables, tried to deal single-handedly with a dispute between striking English coal miners and the HBC, which had employed them.

Unhappy with HBC treatment and lured by the prospect of California gold, the miners began to desert. Largely because of an unfortunate breakdown in communication, two of them were murdered by a group of local Indians. Helmcken sent word back to Fort Victoria that things were getting out of hand. Blanshard hastened to the area and, misjudging the situation, instigated action that eventually resulted in the destruction of an Indian village and execution of the accused killers. Then he returned to Victoria to wait for permission to sail home.

The situation in Victoria had not improved. Certain of the settlement's men, unhappy with Douglas's high-handedness, saw Blanshard as a potential ally who could challenge the chief factor's perceived tyranny. A patient listener, Blanshard agreed to help the colonists write a petition to the British government, outlining their displeasure. Douglas did not approve of Blanshard's fraternizing with the lower rank-and-file and perceived his actions as a blatant disregard of Company rules. Before long there were two parties—Blanshard's, which comprised dissatisfied Company servants, and Douglas's, made up of loyal HBC men. The two men, it seemed, were destined always to be at odds.

It was not a happy time. Blanshard was bitter, disillusioned, and broke. Having a weak constitution, compared to the robust Douglas, he eventually fell victim to a lingering illness triggered by the malaria that had plagued him for many years. Helmcken, called back from Fort Rupert, tried to treat him, with little success. Blanshard became very sick, and in September 1851, when word at last arrived that his resignation had been accepted, he gladly sailed for home, the disgruntled colonists' petition tucked safely into his pocket.

During his time at Fort Victoria, Blanshard had written many reports to London that were highly critical of HBC colonization policy. The

This photo, looking west from Church Hill (present-day site of the Law Courts), shows some of the early construction along Humboldt Street and Burdett Avenue in 1891. The 160-foot light standard is near the foot of an undeveloped Blanshard Street.

Company, he said, had taken all the best land, and the largest tracts, for itself. Land prices were too high for most people, and many, finding they would have to locate far from the fort, had decided to settle elsewhere. Because of this, said Blanshard, there was still no official townsite, just a small village. The colony was slow in developing and the HBC, he declared, was to blame.

Before he left, in a last official duty as governor, he appointed a provisional council—made up of Douglas, HBC retiree John Tod, and petition-signer Captain James Cooper—in an attempt to dilute Douglas's power.

Despite Blanshard's best efforts, Douglas was appointed governor in his place. Soon, under surveyor Joseph Pemberton's expert guidance, the town of Victoria began to take shape. By 1854, houses surrounded the fort and the population, including HBC men at the fort, had swelled to 232.

By that time Blanshard was long gone and is now largely forgotten. He is relegated to the pages of history as the colony's first Royal Governor, remembered in a downtown street that, in recognition of his short and unhappy time here, still carries his name.

Captain James Wright Cooper was one of the three men Blanshard appointed to the provisional council. He was the non-HBC member, a sea captain who owned Bilston Farm in Metchosin. He lived at Thetis Lake when he was not at sea or in England, and hired a friend, Thomas Blinkhorn, to manage his farm.

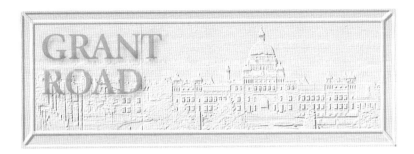

An officer and a gentleman

*D*riving the road to Sooke today, it's impossible to imagine how this area must have looked to its first white settler. Odds are the trees were just as green and the mists hung just as low over the richly forested hills. But today the weary traveller can stop and rest at a red-roofed motel or one of a bevy of Bed-&-Breakfasts along the way. A hundred and fifty years ago there wasn't a pit stop in sight. In fact, there wasn't even a road. When Captain Walter C. Grant left Victoria to go to his newly purchased acreage, the only way to Sooke was by sea.

It was September 1849. Anxious to populate the area around Fort Victoria with gentleman farmers, the Hudson's Bay Company had spread the word in England that wonderful opportunities existed here. Walter Colquhoun Grant took the bait, the first of many to be lured to Vancouver Island by the promise of 100-acre parcels of land at one pound sterling per acre.

A plaque honouring Vancouver Island's first independent settler.

For British men with money, that must have seemed a very fair price indeed. Grant wasn't even deterred by the fact that he'd have to bring his own labourers; he knew he wouldn't have difficulty finding men willing to leave their families and try their luck in the new colony far across the sea.

Grant himself had few ties to the country of his birth. An only child of Scottish parents, he had been orphaned at an early age and raised by relatives in genteel splendour. Inspired by his father, who had been an aide to the Duke of Wellington during the Napoleonic wars, Grant attended military college and by the age of 24 was a captain in the Royal Scots Greys. His future seemed bright until a bank failure cost him a substantial portion of his inheritance. Extravagant by nature and faced with escalating debts, he decided to sell his army commission and make a fresh start with the small amount of capital that remained

J.T. Haverfield depicted Walter Colquhoun Grant's homestead, which he variously called Mullachard and Achaneach after his Scottish ancestral homes. It boasted a palisade and two small cannons, as well as the cricket sets Grant had optimistically brought from England.

The HBC contracted Grant as colonial surveyor, and he readied himself for the journey. Sending his men ahead on the *Harpooner*, Grant chose a more interesting route—the dangerous overland trek across the isthmus of land that separated the Atlantic and Pacific oceans at Panama. Weary from the long voyage around Cape Horn, his men twiddled their thumbs at the fort, unimpressed by their Spartan existence and the meagre pay offered by the HBC in return for their labours. Eventually a canoe glided into the harbour and Captain Grant— first independent settler in the Colony of Vancouver Island—stepped ashore.

Finding that the HBC owned all the choice agricultural land around the settlement, Grant had no option but to look beyond it. James Douglas suggested Metchosin, but Grant had other ideas. He wanted to build a sawmill, which required timber stands and fast-running water, and he wanted to find a spot farther from HBC influence. That spot turned out to be T'sou-ke, or Sooke as we call it today—a place that in 1849 was totally isolated and populated only by people of the Sooke Nation.

Grant's group travelled the 20 miles up the coast in canoes, there being no trail beyond Metchosin. They built dwellings and barns, cleared and cultivated land, raised stock and poultry, and set up a sawmill on a fast-running stream. Grant built a house on the ridge overlooking the harbour. Success seemed assured. But fate—and his own ineptness—got in the way.

Douglas quickly realized that surveying was not Grant's forté and hired Joseph Pemberton in his place. That was fine with Grant, who planned to market his lumber abroad. San Francisco and Hawaii proved far more pleasing to the sophisticated captain than the untamed wildness of his new home, and his trips away from Sooke became more frequent.

In 1854, disillusioned by troubles with his men and high export taxes imposed on his lumber, he sold everything, returned to England, and rejoined the army. A few more years and he might have made it. But by the time the 1858 influx of gold miners fuelled Victoria's fortunes, Grant was far away. He later served in the Crimean War and died of dysentery in India in 1861 at the age of 39.

We have no pictures of Captain Grant, but we do have some interesting images. Young and naive in many ways, a poor manager of men and sadly lacking as a surveyor, he was tall, distinguished, socially acceptable, and pleasant, a bachelor and a man's man who was well liked and well respected at the fort.

Dr. Helmcken called Victoria's first independent settler "a splendid fellow and every inch an officer and a gentleman." Today, all that remains of his time here is the road in Sooke that bears his name, and acre upon acre of broom descended from seeds he brought back from his travels—a brilliant reminder of a colourful character from our past.

In the 1890s, Grant Road was a tranquil country lane leading to one of the coast's most beautiful harbours.

The earliest known photos of Tod House date from the tenure of Fred Pauline and his family. Above, three generations of the Pauline family gathered at the house in the 1890s. The inset photo shows Fred Pauline Sr., and his wife Mary. Fred Pauline Jr. (back row, left above) was a member of the Provincial Legislature (MPP) from 1922-1925.

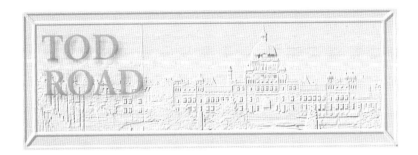

TOD ROAD

Victoria's first retiree

Considering the man it's named for was larger than life, Tod Road is surprisingly small—a quiet surprise that leads east off Cadboro Bay Road, just south of Estevan. Short and narrow, Tod Road is actually more like a country lane. On its north side, unpretentious homes with neat gardens stand obediently, shielded by fences and the occasional hedge; on its south side is a school playing field. Tod Road seems to lead nowhere. But just a couple of blocks to the east as the crow flies is Heron Street, and on the west side of Heron is one of the oldest continuously occupied dwellings in western Canada—the house that Tod built.

Like W.C. Grant before him, John Tod was an early settler in these parts, independent and an individualist. But there the similarity ended. Grant—a young, sophisticated, military man

John Tod and Sophia Lolo Tod

and would-be gentleman farmer—was clearly out of his element in his new surroundings. Tod, on the other hand, with a lifetime of HBC experience behind him, thrived on challenge and adversity. While Grant struggled to tame the wildness of Sooke, 25 miles west of Fort Victoria, Tod leisurely established himself on an equally isolated acreage about five miles to the east of the fort. Tod was the first of many HBC retirees who, after years of arduous adventure at various HBC outposts, came to end his days in peace in the colony on southern Vancouver Island.

Like Grant, Tod had chosen a secluded spot, with only fur trader-farmers and not-so-friendly Indians for company (the Native people at Cadboro Bay were not as welcoming as the Songhees). It is difficult to imagine when you look at the thriving residential area today, but

In 1999, Tod House was still occupied, a small private dwelling in a neighbourhood only a few blocks from the ocean.

in 1851, when Tod first stood on the wood-slat front porch of his six-room, squared-log house, he was lord and master of all he surveyed—a vast expanse of fields and oak trees stretching from just east of the cow trail, south to Tod's stream (later called Bowker Creek), and all along the water-lapped curve of Willows Beach. The road to civilization consisted of a trail that began at the Indian settlement at Cadboro Bay, wound across the countryside through Tod's land, and ended at the east gate of Fort Victoria. Tod would have travelled the five windswept miles to the fort on horseback or by cart—child's play after his long and dangerous journeys across the wilds of New Caledonia.

This was to be a very different existence for the man who, after a poor upbringing in Scotland, had joined the fur trade in his early 20s and served more than 37 years at several different New Caledonia outposts. Tod had quickly become known among HBC men and Indians alike as a dour and difficult fellow with a fiery temper. At one point, getting on the wrong side of Company governor Sir George Simpson cost him nine precious years of his life when he was banished to isolated Fort McLeod with none but the Indians for company. His fierce courage was later to stand him in good stead. Eventually becoming chief trader at Kamloops in the 1840s, it is said that he single-handedly saved Fort Kamloops by threatening to blow up the fort and everything in it—including himself and a group of marauding Indian warriors—with a keg of gunpowder that lay broken open and ready at his feet.

Finally free of the day-to-day battle for survival, Tod settled into his new home and became the quintessential family man. Never lacking female companionship, he had had a succession of wives and companions over the years. Latest of these, a Native woman by the name of Sophia Lolo, was 30 years his junior when they became partners in the mid-1840s. Once established at Oak Bay, she produced five more children to add to his brood. Tod finally married Sophia in 1864, partly to legitimize the status of second daughter Mary, who was about to marry John Bowker, and partly to silence Catherine, a long-ago companion and mother of his son, who had reappeared on the scene claiming to be Mrs. Tod.

Retirement suited John Tod. He was a great party man, and his flute and fiddle were regular features during many lively evenings at his home. Before long, his 406 acres were surrounded on three sides by HBC and other farms.

Tod was also a respected elder statesman in the town of Victoria. Between 1851 and 1858 he served as a member of the legislative council established by Richard Blanshard, and over the next 30 years he continued to be active on the local scene.

John Tod was 88 when he died and was soon joined in Ross Bay Cemetery by Sophia, his last and most devoted wife. Tod House today is designated as a heritage home, too frail for curious feet, visited only during the Old Cemeteries Society's annual Ghost Tours or by appointment. But next time you stroll along Tod Road, Heron Street, or Bowker Place, or gaze out at Mary Tod Island from the foot of Bowker Avenue, pause for a moment and remember John Tod—our first and most famous retiree.

HELMCKEN ROAD

Dr. Heal-my-skin

The most familiar part of Helmcken Road is a busy modern thoroughfare that runs north from Old Island Highway, over the Trans-Canada Highway, and across Burnside to merge with Wilkinson just south of Interurban. But if you turn *south* from Old Island Highway onto the block of Helmcken that leads toward Esquimalt Harbour, speed bumps remind you: "Slow down—you're approaching Victoria's past!"

Helmcken comes to an abrupt halt at View Royal Avenue, but a short path leads you to a wooden staircase and the small deck above Limekiln Cove. Rest awhile on one of the wooden benches as you look southward over the sheltered bay where Old Country ships once stopped to replenish their water supply, and remember the man this street was named for over a century ago.

Dr. John Sebastian Helmcken was one of 80 immigrants—mostly coal miners and labourer-settlers—sent by the Hudson's Bay Company to its new outpost on Vancouver Island in 1850. Born in London to German parents some 25 years earlier, Helmcken had overcome his humble beginnings, studied medicine, and become a qualified physician.

A medical practitioner, politician, and family man, J.S. Helmcken enjoyed a long and distinguished career.

Helmcken House (above) has survived as one of Victoria's heritage sites and sits beside the Royal British Columbia Museum in the spot where it was built. Over the years it was enlarged to accommodate a growing family. The original house is the section on the right. It was built on land given to Helmcken by his father-in-law and neighbour, Governor James Douglas, when Helmcken married Douglas's oldest daughter, Cecelia (left).

He was an adventurous fellow, anxious to see the world, and the HBC provided the perfect opportunity. He signed up and sailed around Cape Horn on the *Norman Morison*. It was a long and hazardous voyage. Helmcken must have breathed a sigh of relief when the ship reached port, and he prepared to meet the man who would figure so largely in his future.

Helmcken's first impressions of James Douglas, who had returned to Fort Victoria from Fort Vancouver the year before, were far from favourable. Douglas, he wrote later, "was of very grave disposition…cold and unimpassioned." But Douglas's family members were more agreeable, and one in particular young Cecilia—caught his eye.

Cecilia was James and Amelia's oldest surviving child. At fifteen she had her mother's dark complexion and black eyes and a graceful figure. Two years later, after a dangerous and

In 1856, Vancouver Island's first elected legislative assembly included Dr. Helmcken, front row centre, and clockwise from him: Thomas Skinner, Joseph McKay, Joseph Pemberton, Joseph Porter (legislative clerk), and James Yates.

arduous assignment at Fort Rupert (near present-day Port McNeill), Helmcken pleaded with the HBC for a passage home to England. But when he arrived at Fort Victoria and found Cecilia—now a beautiful young woman of seventeen—awaiting him, all thoughts of leaving went out of his mind.

They were married at the fort on December 27, 1852, in the middle of a snowstorm that almost ruined the wedding. In those days the Church of England stipulated that weddings must be performed before midday. The only carriage in town, a two-wheeled light cart, was rendered useless by the snow, and by the time a substitute—a dry-goods box set on willow runners—was produced, it was getting perilously close to noon. Fortunately the bridal party appeared just in time. As the clock struck twelve, the ring was placed on Cecilia's finger and the Helmckens took their place in Victoria's history.

They set up house on a one-acre parcel of land given to them by Cecilia's parents, who lived next door. The good doctor was enormously popular, always smiling, and never refused to treat people who couldn't afford to pay. Children, who called him "Doctor Heal my-skin," loved him, and he surrounded himself with children of his own. Two died in infancy and were buried in the Helmcken House garden. Then Cecilia died of a chill at the age of 30, soon after giving birth to a child who perished three weeks later. Cecilia, her last-born, and the coffins of the two babies that had died earlier were placed together in a brick vault at the Old Burying Ground on Quadra Street. Four children lived to mourn them.

Dr. Helmcken buried himself in politics. First Speaker of the Vancouver Island General Assembly, he later helped negotiate the colony's union with Canada before leaving public life in favour of his work and family. He eventually retired from medicine in 1910 at the age of 86.

True to Cecilia's memory, he never remarried, but doted on his surviving children and grandchildren. An 1894 addition to his little log house made room for daughter Dolly and her husband, who looked after him till his death, at 96, in 1920. By that time the Old Burying Ground had been closed for 48 years, but special permission was given for Cecilia's vault to be opened, and his ashes were placed inside it. Helmcken House, where he and his family had shared such happy times, stands where it was built in the 1850s and is still open to the public today.

Many years earlier, Dr. Helmcken had bought 300 acres of farmland in what is now View Royal. His land stretched northwards from what was once called Helmcken Cove up to and beyond Deadman's (Craigflower) Creek. The doctor is long gone, but his legacy lives on in the road that bears his name.

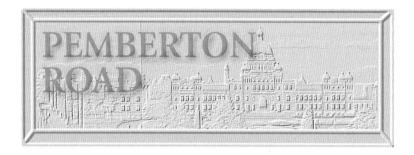

PEMBERTON ROAD

The man who created Victoria

*I*n today's busy downtown Victoria, it's a pleasure to find a road that preserves the peaceful feeling of days gone by. Turning sharply away from frenetic Fort Street, Pemberton Road meanders slowly south toward Rockland Avenue. A walk along its tree-lined sidewalks with their mix of apartments and old houses is an opportunity to muse for awhile about the man who quite literally created the Victoria we know today.

Joseph Despard Pemberton was an Irish-born civil engineer who had successfully built roadways in Ireland and England. At 30 years old and ready for adventure, he decided to head for the far side of Canada when he heard that the Hudson's Bay Company planned to colonize Vancouver Island and was looking for a qualified surveyor. He applied and was immediately accepted. Shortly after, he set sail from Southampton.

It was a miserable trip. Ill with malaria and exhausted by the long voyage around Cape Horn, Pemberton was happy to disembark at Esquimalt at the end of June 1851—and unhappy

Joseph Despard Pemberton

with the final stage of the journey to his new home. The three-mile road from Esquimalt to Fort Victoria was, in his own words, "execrable." But his eyes must have been gleaming at the prospect of the work that lay ahead.

With the help of Benjamin William Pearse, his assistant and lifelong friend, Pemberton mapped out a plan of action. Within four months the two men had completed a preliminary survey of Vancouver Island's coastline and mapped out the HBC land surrounding the fort. At that time, all settlement centred around the outpost, which had been extended since 1843 to accommodate new arrivals.

The HBC instructed Pemberton to prepare a town plan and a general structure for colonization that would reproduce the class divisions of England. In other words, said the HBC, land cost should be such as to discourage squatters, paupers, and land speculators.

Pemberton set to work, designing a plan that would achieve settlement within the town of Victoria and the development of farming in the outer areas. His three-tier system comprised town

Joseph Pemberton's "Gonzales" was on the hillside overlooking Ross Bay and the Strait of Juan de Fuca. It was the scene of lively parties, thrown by one of the area's largest private landowners.

lots, suburban lots, and country lots. Retiring HBC employees were enticed to the area with the promise of 20 acres of farming land, courtesy of the Company, if they agreed to settle there.

Government Street became the first street in British North America west of the Rockies. The rolling meadows and forested areas that Douglas had earmarked for public use became Beacon Hill Park. Pemberton's town plan included schools and churches. He also insisted on preserving stands of trees, both for their beauty and for the protection they afforded against strong winds from the south.

Pemberton later travelled to Saanich, Sooke, Cowichan, Nanaimo, Qualicum, and the Alberni Valley, boldly going where no white man had gone before and returning exhilarated by his adventures. He also surveyed parts of the Lower Mainland. The area around the town of Pemberton is just one of the legacies of a man who made his mark in British Columbia's history.

Back in Victoria, Pemberton decided to build a real home to replace the log structure on the large tract of land he'd acquired in earlier days. With holdings that included the lower part of Fernwood and almost all of Oak Bay—by the late 1850s he was the area's largest private landowner—Pemberton was hardly at a loss for a location. In 1885 he built a mansion high on a hillside at one corner of his 1200-acre farm. The huge house had twenty rooms, five bathrooms, billiard room, conservatory, library, and a glorious southward view. Pemberton and his elegant, aristocratic wife, Teresa, whom he'd married in England in 1864, entertained at "Gonzales" on a grand scale. Their dinners, balls, and garden parties enhanced Victoria's social scene.

Described as cheery, bright, amiable, affectionate, and well respected by all who knew him, Pemberton was a member of the first elected legislative assembly before leaving government service to concentrate on business and agriculture. He later came out of semi-retirement to design Oak Bay Avenue, which passed through his property. The avenue would figure prominently in his future, for at the age of 71 he died suddenly of a massive heart attack while riding his horse near what is now the Oak Bay Junction. He is buried, with his family, in Ross Bay Cemetery.

"Gonzales" stood for 67 years on St. Charles Street, just below Rockland, until the city eventually surrounded and swallowed it. It was demolished in 1952. All that remains of its owner today are Pemberton and Despard—the nearby streets that still bear his name.

Pemberton's 1852 town plan formed the basis for residential neighbourhoods like this one. Richard Maynard, one of Victoria's early professional photographers, took this view northeast from Christ Church Cathedral in the early 1870s. The Quadra Street Burying Ground is at right centre.

All in a day's Wark

Victoria's Wark Street hiccups its way north from Queens, crosses Bay, cuts off at Kings, then picks up briefly again at Hillside, only to come to an abrupt halt at Market. It's a remarkably short reminder of someone who once owned all of the Hillside area, yet the street's stops and starts seem to mirror the life of the man who considered Victoria a jewel in the crown of a colourful career.

In 1792, while Vancouver and Quadra were celebrating the naming of this island at Nootka Sound, a family in County Donegal, Ireland, was welcoming its latest addition—a son they named John. John Wark—or Work, as the Hudson's Bay Company insisted on calling him— soon found his homeland too small for his adventurous soul. Running away from home at fourteen, he joined the North West Company in 1814 and served in the eastern part of Canada for eight years. In 1822, after the North West and Hudson's Bay companies had merged, he

John and Josette Work

was sent by the HBC to Washington Territory to establish a Company farm at Fort Colvile. There, on the Columbia River just south of Nelson, B.C., in an area now flooded by the Roosevelt Dam, he met the girl who was to become his wife.

Josette Legace was the daughter of a Spokane Indian woman and a French voyageur. She was only fourteen when she married Work, who was twenty years her senior, "in the custom of the country." The marriage was, like James Douglas's and John Tod's, sanctioned by the HBC, which recognized the undeniable advantage of having its fur traders marry Indian women. The Company even covered Work's wedding expenses, stipulating in return that the bride must accompany him on all HBC trips into Columbia Territory.

Whatever the reasons for the union, it seems to have been a happy one. Josette accompanied her husband on most of his trips from that time forward and proved a loyal and

Josette Work is shown with two of her ten surviving children (left), Suzette and David. The photo of the Works' home (below) was taken in the 1880s, after John Work's death, but it shows how Hillside was still a rural area at the time. The people in the photograph are unidentified.

devoted partner. They had many adventures together. When Work was made chief trader, Josette accompanied him on trading journeys that took them more than a thousand miles over land and water. Their children, born along the way, learned first-hand what life in a fur-trading family was all about.

Travelling through the Sacramento Valley, then up the coast to Fort Vancouver, Work moved north to Fort Simpson (near present-day Prince Rupert) in 1834 and began trading in Alaska, the Queen Charlottes, and elsewhere. In 1836 Josette and the children joined him. Horrified by the despairing and helpless attitude of Native women in the area, Josette became a willing, patient, and dedicated teacher, showing the girls and young women how to cook and sew and how to keep themselves neat and clean, inspiring them to build for themselves a better life.

Work never took his wife's efforts for granted and indeed held her in great esteem. In 1841, when they had been together for fifteen years, he penned his feelings for her in a letter thus: "The little wife and I get on very well. She is to me an affectionate partner, simple and uninstructed though she is, and takes good care of my children and myself."

His feelings toward her never changed.

Work adored his family, and was never happier than when he was around them. His was a large brood, as were so many others at that time. Josette had never let pregnancy or the birth of another baby interfere with sharing her husband's life and travels, but she must have looked forward to his retirement with pleasure.

Life had not been easy. Somewhere along the way, like John Tod before him, Work had managed to run afoul of an HBC officer—in

Work's case, Chief Factor John McLoughlin—and had spent some years in isolation at Fort Simpson. For a while, his career was on hold. Then McLoughlin retired and Work's star began to rise again.

By 1846, now a chief factor himself and still stationed at Fort Simpson, Work was beginning to slow down and feeling decidedly the worse for wear. He and Josette discussed the future. Though he had always supposed he would one day return to the country of his birth, Work realized that Josette—West Coast born and bred—would not be happy in a strange land across the sea. Victoria seemed a splendid compromise.

Finding that, as an HBC man, he could pretty well pick whatever land he liked, Work chose a large tract, which he called Hillside, settled his family upon it in 1849, and joined them in 1852.

You would think he'd be ready for a bit of peace and quiet, but it wasn't to be. No sooner had he arrived in Victoria than James Douglas insisted that he join the legislative council established by former governor Richard Blanshard a few months earlier. Appointed governor in Blanshard's place, Douglas proceeded to expand the three-man council, originally made up of himself, John Tod, and James Cooper, to include Roderick Finlayson and now Work.

Despite his better judgment, for he had little taste for politics, Work took his place in the small group that, against Blanshard's wishes, now had a majority HBC presence, and he set to work developing his farm. Responsibility weighed heavily on him. In a letter to a friend he said, "With nearly three scores on my shoulders, the effects of old age must be expected and I feel

Thirty years after John Work's death, Victoria refocused on Hillside for another reason.
The new Hillside Jail opened in 1886 under the direction of this earnest group.
Left to right: Guard Joseph Mellon, Gaoler Robert Liddell, Head Guard Almond Thomas,
Warden R.F. John, Head Gaoler William Muldoon, Guard H. Blake, and Gaoler E.J. Parsons.

them coming on me fast and ought to have settled at some quiet place before now, but my large family and narrow means induce me to hang on, but I assure you it is with some reluctance." Retirement, it seemed, would have to wait.

No stranger to farming, Work threw himself into clearing and cultivating the land. He successfully grew all manner of fruits and vegetables and was particularly renowned for his prize pumpkins, some of which weighed in excess of 100 pounds. Starting with 700 acres, Work eventually owned more than 1300, and the boundaries of his property reached from the Gorge to Cook Street and from Finlayson to Kings.

As well as becoming a prime food producer for the fort, Hillside Farm became the social hub of Victoria. Its owners were wonderful hosts, and guests were always welcome. Starved for female company, the men of Victoria revelled in the Works' hospitality and even more so in the affections of their eight pretty daughters. No matter that their two surviving sons—a third had died at the age of twelve—amounted to little; the daughters more than made up for them.

All married well, but three became the wives of men who would be prominent in B.C. history. Sarah's husband, Roderick Finlayson, later became mayor of the city; Jane and her husband, Dr. William Fraser Tolmie, became the parents of B.C.'s first native-born premier; and Suzette's husband, Edward Gawler Prior, served as the province's premier and then its lieutenant governor.

The Works' own union had been blessed by the church some years previously, and by the time he died at Hillside in December 1861, still in the employ of the HBC, they had been together for 35 years. He left an incredible record of service. Although entitled to regular time off, he had not taken leave in almost five decades. During his time as a legislative council member, he missed only two of more than 100 meetings. At 70 years of age, he was the oldest man in B.C. when illness claimed his life. He was buried in the Quadra Street Burying Ground, just a few blocks south of his home. Josette, who was much respected by the community, was the oldest person in the province when she died in 1896, at the age of 87. She is buried at Ross Bay Cemetery.

The family lives on in our city today in a group of streets around Hillside Avenue—Josette, John, David, Henry, Graham, Prior, Blackwood, and Jackson—and in the smallest street with the biggest history, the one named after the man who built Hillside, all in a day's Wark.

True founder of Victoria

*I*t's no surprise that Finlayson Street runs from west to east a couple of blocks north of Hillside. Just before Christmas 1849, Roderick Finlayson married Sarah, daughter of Hillside Farm owner John Work, so the proximity mirrors the family connection.

What *is* surprising, however, is the shortness of the street. Running only a few blocks, from Douglas to Cedar Hill, it hardly reflects the length of this illustrious man's career.

Roderick Finlayson was born in 1818 at Ross-shire, Scotland, and was only nineteen when he came to Canada, via New York, in 1837. He found work with the Hudson's Bay Company as an apprentice clerk and travelled by birchbark canoe to his first posting on the Ottawa River. In 1839 he headed across Canada to the Columbia Territory west of the Rocky Mountains. At Fort Nisqually, at the head of Puget Sound, he met with James Douglas. Together, the two embarked in the *Beaver* for Russian territory,

Roderick Finlayson

north of the 54th parallel. On the way, they passed Vancouver Island. Finlayson later remarked, "I little thought that it would ultimately be my home."

After completing business at Sitka with the Russian America Fur Company, the party moved on to Fort Durham where, in 1840, Finlayson was left as second-in-command. His time there was punctuated by several harrowing incidents involving hostile Natives. At one point the fort was besieged for several days until the Indians, realizing that trade was more profitable than war, made peace with Finlayson by handing over a large bundle of furs.

By 1842 Finlayson was employed at Fort Simpson, and it was here that his life was changed by an encounter with Sarah Jane, daughter of the chief factor, John Work. But in June 1843 he and his love were parted when Finlayson was transferred to the new Company post on the southern tip of Vancouver Island.

Fort Victoria was not far from the Songhees village—within cannon range, as shown in this photo looking west from the fort in the 1860s. The brick building on the right was one of the first constructed in Victoria's downtown, and it still stands at the foot of Fort Street.

Having established the new outpost at Fort Victoria, James Douglas was ready to return to Fort Vancouver. He placed Charles Ross in charge of construction of the new fort, with Finlayson as second-in-command. Unfortunately Charles Ross was not long for this world. In early 1844 he became very sick. Blaming "a rather merry Christmas and New Year," which, he decided, had made things worse, he continued to decline through the spring. In June, after five days of terrible suffering, he died. Finlayson, who had ministered to him during those last, agonizing hours, took command of the fort. He was just 26 years old.

Almost immediately his skills were tested by an altercation with a group of Songhees people living on the waterfront north of the fort.

Apparently they had killed some Company oxen, and when Finlayson demanded payment, the Songhees chief responded by gathering together an angry group that promptly proceeded to shower the fort with bullets.

Finlayson, having ascertained that one of the Indian lodges was vacant, blew it to smithereens with grapeshot from one of the fort's nine-pounders. The Indians were frightened by the noisy, devastating display—and very much impressed. When Finlayson assured the chief that he would have no qualms about destroying the entire Indian village, payment for the oxen was immediately produced and peace was restored.

The young man remained in control of the fort until Douglas returned permanently in 1849, and many consider him the true founder

The Victoria landscape was constantly changing as the city grew. Roderick Finlayson's grand home on Douglas Street (above), just south of Bay, did not survive long into the twentieth century, but it lasted longer than this cascade near Government Street, which in the 1860s was named Finlayson Falls (below).

of Victoria. Douglas himself described Finlayson as a man with "energy, perseverance, method and sound judgment…a young man of great probity and high moral worth," and although they would disagree on many occasions, Douglas always held him in high regard.

With Douglas back in charge, Finlayson became chief accountant and first treasurer for the colonial government, and when the Work family arrived at their new Hillside property, he was able at last to marry his beloved Sarah. The newlyweds celebrated their first New Year as man and wife in their quarters on the Wharf Street side of the fort. In the late 1850s they moved into a huge home on Douglas Street, at the centre of a property that stretched from Rock Bay across to Spring Ridge (the northern part of today's Fernwood). Their five sons and four daughters enjoyed living way out in the country, in a big, spacious house set amidst meadows, orchards, and formal gardens, with carriage houses, stables, and a barn for the cow.

Sarah was a good soul who loved children and helped others whenever she could. In 1864, when Dr. Helmcken's wife Cecilia became ill with pneumonia and died, it was Sarah who took charge of Cecilia's newborn son, who died a few days later. Like her parents before her, Sarah was a wonderful hostess, and when Finlayson became mayor of Victoria in 1878, the big Douglas Street house was a centre for entertainment in the little city.

Finlayson was also a member of the legislative assembly for many years. A very successful businessman, he remained active until the day he died, suddenly, in January 1892, when he was 74 years old. The whole city was in mourning. Pallbearers at his funeral included Dr. John Helmcken and Joseph Pemberton. He was buried at Ross Bay.

Sarah lived on in their Douglas Street home. Shortly after she died in 1906, the beautiful old house disappeared in favour of commercial development, and a goodly chunk of Victoria's history disappeared along with it.

Finlayson was the last surviving HBC man from the 1840s in Victoria, and his death marked the end of an era. An adventurer in the truest sense of the word, he is remembered today in Finlayson Arm, in channels and islands around our coast—and in that rather short street named after one of our city's greatest citizens and early pioneers.

The forgotten farmer

Buried deep in the heart of Esquimalt is a road running between Fairview and Dominion, just south of the E&N Railway line, that tells the tale of a once-promising Puget's Sound Agricultural Company (PSAC) enterprise. Viewfield Road follows, for a short while, the boundary of the earliest PSAC farm. Not far to the southwest, Macaulay Street records the name of the man who was hired to manage that farm.

Formed in 1840 as the "farming arm" of the Hudson's Bay Company, PSAC had enjoyed considerable success with its Columbia River and Fort Langley operations. But after 1846, when all territory south of the 49th parallel became American-owned, PSAC's fortunes changed. Fort Langley, Uplands Farm, and the dairies around Fort Victoria could not make up the production shortfall, and PSAC decided to develop farms on the southern tip of Vancouver Island.

In 1850, Viewfield Farm was founded, and as its name suggests, its 600 acres encompassed some of the finest views in Esquimalt. Its southern border followed the shoreline from West Bay to Kanaka Bay, encompassing Work Point, Macaulay Point, and Saxe Point. Its western boundary started at Kanaka Bay, cut across the sea end of Admirals Road, then ran to a point near the top of the hill on Old Esquimalt Road. Its eastern boundary passed from West Bay to the Victoria City-Esquimalt line, present-day Dominion Road. To the north, Viewfield's common boundary with Constance Cove Farm, another PSAC property, ran in a straight line along the ridge above Old Esquimalt Road.

At the western boundary of Viewfield, where the foot of Constance Avenue is today, Kanaka Farm was worked by a small colony of native Hawaiian Islanders (Kanakas) who had come to this coast with the fur traders.

The Viewfield Farm bailiff was closest to the fort by name and by nature. Donald Macaulay was a Scot, like so many of the HBC officers of that time. And unlike the other PSAC bailiffs who followed, Macaulay was a Company employee of long standing. After travelling across the mountains to the West Coast around 1834, he had served on the HBC brig *Llama* for a few years and had then been stationed at Fort Simpson.

In 1850 PSAC appointed him bailiff of the first of four farms to be established on ten square miles of land selected for the Company by James Douglas. The appointment was deliberate.

Having an HBC man manage the first farm would, it was thought, save time and enable the farm to be up and running in short order.

By the time the Macaulays moved to Esquimalt, the family included four daughters, all of whom were baptized at Fort Victoria by Reverend Robert Staines. Two more daughters were born while they were at Viewfield.

Macaulay was a man of few words, who didn't see the need to waste time on cultivating friendly relationships with his neighbours. The sign above the entrance to his farm was short and to the point: "All drivellers who drivel this way, man, woman or child—please shut the gate." There are no pictures of the fellow, but Dr. J.S. Helmcken later described him as "a highlander or crofter, a most trustworthy man…long and spare."

Trustworthy he may have been, and clearly not given to the excesses that eventually proved to be the downfall of at least one of his fellow farmers. But despite his head start, Donald Macaulay didn't have much success with Viewfield. According to Douglas's census of the white population four years after Macaulay arrived, Viewfield Farm still only boasted fourteen people, nine of whom were children under fifteen. Three dwelling houses were recorded. Chief products listed were sheep and wool, some horses, cattle and oxen, seven milk cows, and a few pigs. Only 35 of the 600 acres had been cleared.

Admittedly, making the rocky, densely forested land in this area suitable for farming was a huge challenge. Felling the trees was but the first step. That left a maze of pine stumps with thick roots that had to be cut out, and then the stumps had to be rolled away and burned. As Dr. Helmcken recalled later about his own land, "The stumps…never seemed to rot. I have seen them pretty solid after 20 years!"

By 1860 Macaulay and his family were ready to return to Fort Simpson. Two of the Macaulay daughters had married while the family was at Viewfield. The oldest, Mary, wed Captain William McNeill Jr. in 1853, and they lived in

From 1878 to 1956, the fort at Macaulay Point was part of a coast artillery defense system designed to protect our harbour. Richard Maynard took this photo of the military fortifications under construction in 1878.

Sarah Lindley Crease depicted the rolling fields of Macaulay Plains in 1898, before they were covered by army buildings during World War Two.

a comfortable home at McNeill or Shoal Bay. Two years later Flora, the second oldest, married James, son of John Tod, the HBC retiree who had settled in Oak Bay five years earlier.

In 1863 Donald Macaulay returned to Victoria to take charge of the HBC powder magazine at Esquimalt. In 1868 he was accidentally drowned in Esquimalt Harbour when a munitions barge sprung a leak.

By that time, Viewfield Farm's 600 acres of promise were almost forgotten. Eventually Victoria spread west to cover it. At the outbreak of World War Two, Macaulay Plains disappeared under army buildings. Macaulay Point was fortified. The farm's flat lands near Work Point Barracks became the site of wartime housing for shipbuilders and their families.

Eclipsed by the social and other shenanigans of the three bailiffs who followed him to the Esquimalt area, the efforts of Donald Macaulay have gone largely unrecognized. Macaulay Street still runs south from Esquimalt Road in the direction of Macaulay Point, but the only reminder of Viewfield Farm today is a tiny street just north of West Bay that still bears its name.

A touch of class

*T*oday, Langford Street doglegs its way west from the Point Ellice Bridge, coming to a grinding halt after about eight blocks—and a good few kilometres short of the area settled by the man it is named after. Fortunately it's not the only reminder of a fellow and his family who made an enormous impact on Victoria in those long-ago days.

Captain Edward Edwards Langford was the second of the four bailiffs appointed by PSAC to develop farms in the Esquimalt area. He was an interesting charac- ter, a retired army officer from the south of England and a distant rela- tive of Governor Richard Blanshard. Langford was intrigued by the prospect of being a gentleman farmer and was more than adequately prepared

Flora and Edward Langford

to play the part. But when the supply ship *Tory* pulled into the harbour on May 10, 1851—just one year after Blanshard's own arrival—Langford was in for a rude awakening.

It should have been a momentous occasion. After all, Langford's was the first white family to arrive at the fort direct from England. Indeed, the fashionably dressed Langford ladies in their crinolined, caped, and bonneted London finery occasioned open-mouthed amazement among HBC men and Natives alike as they made their way gaily from the landing place to the fort. In those early days, beautiful young ladies were few and far between.

But delight at reaching their destination soon turned to dismay at the primitive conditions that awaited them. All that had been pro- vided for Langford, his family, and the farm helpers he'd brought with him were two rough log huts, each with a sin- gle room. Langford was furious. Accustomed as they were to comfort verging on luxury, he, his very pregnant wife, and their five daughters absolutely could not be expected to live in such totally inadequate surroundings! Langford considered himself personally insulted by Chief Factor James Douglas and the HBC,

"Colwood," home of the Langfords, was built in 1851 at the northwest corner of 600-acre Colwood farm, where the Royal Colwood Golf Course is today. The painting above, by Edward Parker Bedwell, shows it shortly after construction. The photo below was taken much later.

and he complained bitterly about the Company and its policies for the rest of his days.

The immediate accommodation problem was addressed with the help of the wife of the Company chaplain, who invited the Langfords to share their generous-sized quarters. Shortly afterward, when the birth of Flora Langford's sixth child was imminent, Governor Blanshard came to the rescue. Waiting for formal acceptance of his resignation and permission to leave the colony, he was still in residence a few hundred yards north of the fort and, with typical chivalry, offered to share his modest abode with the grateful mother-to-be. George Richard Langford, who made his appearance soon afterward in the home of the first governor of Vancouver Island, was the first white male child to be born in the colony.

Roderick Finlayson had surveyed the area that would comprise Captain Langford's farm some four years earlier, and a sawmill had been built just north of it. Langford took over supervision of the 600-acre property, known as Mill Farm or Esquimalt Farm, and renamed it Colwood Farm. An odd-shaped piece of land, its boundary stretched westward from Paterson Point to the northeast corner of the old Hatley Park estate, across to the far end of Colwood Lake, then north to Mill Stream, skirting the mill as it followed the stream back to the harbour.

Indians, Kanakas, and Langford's own men felled trees and cleared land. The Langfords' residence, called "Colwood" after their old home in Sussex, was built at the farthest end of the property from the fort. With Flora Langford as its charming host, "Colwood" soon became a centre of social activity. The colony's first independent settler, Captain W.C. Grant of

Sooke, was a frequent visitor, as were Navy men from the ships that anchored in Esquimalt Harbour. Riding parties, picnics, and dances were frequent attractions at "Colwood," and the naval officers responded with invitations of their own to social occasions aboard ship. Not surprisingly, several of the Langford girls ended up marrying Navy men.

An unmarried sister of Captain Langford sailed out from England to join the family. She was a trained teacher, and her Academy for Young Ladies, built by Captain Langford close to the family home, was attended by the daughters of several HBC officials, including Agnes and Alice Douglas. Elegant dwellings, flower gardens, fashionable clothes, and good manners were hallmarks of this family's presence. The Langfords, it seemed, had carved a civilized niche for themselves in the rough-and-ready environment of the new colony.

Unfortunately, appearances to the contrary, all was not well on the western shores of Esquimalt Harbour. Captain Langford had taken the "gentleman" part of being a gentleman farmer very seriously indeed, but the "farmer" component left a lot to be desired. His agreement with PSAC stipulated that, as bailiff, he was entitled to Company-paid expenses until his farm showed a profit, but that day never came. While the expenses piled up—and in one year, "groceries" might include several gallons of rum, sherry, and brandy—revenues were lacking.

To make matters worse, Langford's ongoing feud with Governor Douglas showed no signs of a resolution. Casting himself as unofficial "leader of the opposition," Langford was a constant thorn in Douglas's side. Complaints about Douglas's leadership, the HBC, and the colonial government rained upon the London office of the Secretary of State. Locally, Langford found a sympathizer in Captain Grant, who also felt badly done to by Douglas. Grant later surveyed Langford Lake and Langford Plains, naming them in his friend's honour.

In 1861, unable to tolerate the oppressive HBC regime any longer, Langford gathered his family together and returned to England. He may not have made much of an impression on James Douglas, but the local newspaper praised him in passing. He had, said the *Colonist*, "done much to soften the rude features of pioneer life" and had introduced "the tone of modern English society" to the colony.

His daughters are remembered in ports, creeks, points, and basins around our coast. The family name, it seems, is everywhere. As you drive through Vic West or Colwood, swing a club on the Colwood Golf Course, or travel through the Langford area, spare a thought for the would-be gentleman farmer who played a small but significant role in Victoria's past.

A gentleman and a farmer

Just north of Langford Street in Vic West is Skinner Street, a brief continuation of Craigflower Road not too far from what used to be the northeast border of Thomas Skinner's farm. Short on street length but long on performance, Skinner was the only successful farmer in the Esquimalt area a century and a half ago.

In January 1853, almost three years after it brought Dr. John Helmcken to these shores, the *Norman Morison* carried two Puget's Sound Agricultural Company bailiffs and 25 families of farmers, labourers, carpenters, blacksmiths, and servants to the mouth of Esquimalt Harbour.

It had been an unusually rough voyage, with hurricanes around Cape Horn and appalling sailing weather on the approach to Vancouver Island. After five gruelling months at sea, Mary Skinner, who was expecting her sixth child, must have been particularly relieved to reach dry land and the prospect of the comfortable home that awaited them.

Realizing that his wife needed to rest, Skinner kept his family on board an extra night. When they reached the fort the next day, however, there was no sign of the house PSAC had promised, and by this time all available

accommodations at the fort had been taken by their shipmates. All that was left for the seven Skinners and their three servants was a one-room shack on Kanaka Row (now Humboldt Street) that had to be swept before the family could move in. A few weeks later Mary Skinner gave birth to a third daughter, Constance. Only a Hudson's Bay blanket separated the delivering mother from the shack's other occupants.

Like the Langfords, the Skinners had been specially chosen by PSAC because of their perceived ability to form the basis of a respectable establishment on Vancouver Island. Indeed, Thomas Skinner was more than qualified for the role of gentleman farmer. A highborn native of West Thurrock, in Essex, he had performed well with the English branch of the East India Company, and PSAC had wasted no time in offering him a position.

Constance Cove Farm was on the opposite side of Esquimalt Harbour and due east of Captain Langford's Colwood Farm. It was tucked in beside Viewfield Farm, where Donald Macaulay had settled three years earlier. The Constance Cove Farm boundary followed the Gorge waterfront from Selkirk Water to just west of today's Tillicum Road, then cut through the middle of the Gorge Vale Golf Course and took

Thomas and Mary Skinner with five of their eight children in the 1860s, shortly before they left Esquimalt to make a new start in the Cowichan Valley as independent farmers. Constance (standing at right) was born in a Kanaka Row shack soon after they arrived in Victoria.

in a small stretch of Esquimalt waterfront at Constance Cove before running almost due east back toward Selkirk Water. Between them, Constance Cove and Viewfield farms comprised most of present-day Esquimalt.

Wagons overturned or got stuck on the rough road through the woods from the fort to Rowe's stream (now Millstream), so building materials for the Skinner's new home had to be sent by freight canoe up the Gorge or by sea around to Esquimalt Harbour. Eventually a comfortable house was built on an oak-studded slope above a sheltered cove, close to where the naval vessels tied up.

By his second year, Skinner's 600 acres were producing potatoes, turnips, wheat, and barley. Constance Cove was also the only farm producing butter. "Oaklands," the huge family home, had been joined by nine dwelling houses, and a total of 34 people lived on Skinner's land.

Seeing the farm as an excellent trading venue, PSAC built storage warehouses on the waterfront at Skinner's Cove. Beef, bacon, butter, wheat, and flour were loaded onto trading ships, many bound for Russian Sitka. When British naval vessels en route to the Crimean War called in at Esquimalt for supplies, Thomas Skinner's farm was ready to serve them.

A view of Skinner Street looking towards the city of Victoria in 1945.

Like the young Langford ladies, the Skinner girls were a source of delight to fort officers and naval men alike. Afternoon tea, parties, dances, skating, riding, boating on the Gorge, and musical and theatre shows were the order of the day. "Oaklands," with its lovely, trellis-fence-enclosed English country garden, was the scene of many a burgeoning romance, and "good" marriages between the house's young occupants and naval officers were almost guaranteed.

In 1856 Skinner was one of Esquimalt's two members elected to the first legislative assembly. By this time Skinner had joined the group of disgruntled colonists who complained bitterly about the Douglas administration. Douglas, they said, was unable to distinguish between his role as governor and his position as chief factor and seemed to use both to his own advantage.

(Two years later Douglas relinquished his HBC position when he became governor of the new colony of British Columbia.)

In the mid-1860s the HBC, disillusioned by poor returns from the four farms, took over PSAC assets. Skinner was forced to move from Esquimalt to the Cowichan Valley, where he had purchased land earlier with a view to becoming an independent farmer.

For the second time in eleven years, the Skinners started afresh. Their eight children, accustomed to a sizzling social life at the comfortable "Oaklands," found themselves living in tents while their new home, "Farleigh," was being built. Instead of pony rides and canoe trips up the Gorge, they milked cows and churned butter. Cowichan and Esquimalt were worlds apart.

On November 13, 1940, Mary Skinner was at a ceremony unveiling a cairn describing the history of Craigflower School. The daughter of Thomas Skinner was probably one of the early pupils there. At right is Alexander Watson, grandson of Kenneth McKenzie, under whose supervision the school was built.

Not surprisingly, the older girls soon married and left the Valley. Constance, whose life had begun in that humble shack on Kanaka Row, married a young Victoria lawyer and politician, Alexander Davie. Davie later became premier of the province and attorney general. In 1889, at the peak of his political career, he died suddenly at the age of 43. Constance's father, Thomas Skinner, died the same year. Mary died several years later.

Thomas and Mary are buried in Quamichan, at St. Peter's Church. Constance Cove Farm is long gone, but the Skinner name lives on in that small portion of road—an all-too-brief reminder of a man who distinguished himself by being the only successful farmer in that once-uncultivated area west of the Johnson Street bridge.

Home of the McKenzies

As you travel the built-up length of today's Craigflower Road, you may find it hard to picture it as a winding trail leading west from Fort Victoria. But where it intersects with Admirals Road and becomes the Island Highway, pause for a moment (if you're lucky enough to have a red light) and take a quick look around. On the northwest corner is the former home of the man who gave Craigflower its name—Kenneth McKenzie.

McKenzie was born the son of a surgeon in Edinburgh in 1811. His first experience with farming was managing his father's estate. He did well, but the depression of the 1840s ruined many such an enterprise, and when McKenzie's father died in 1844, the property was in debt. By the time it could be sold, McKenzie was 41 and ready for a fresh challenge.

The Puget's Sound Agricultural Company was impressed with McKenzie's enthusiasm and experience. Seeing him as the ideal man to oversee the largest of the four farms it was establishing in the Esquimalt area, PSAC offered him a five-year contract, free passage, and a share in the farm's profits.

Needing no further incentive, McKenzie recruited labourers, blacksmiths, carpenters, ploughmen, smiths, servant girls, and a schoolmaster. In August 1852, he and his family set sail on the *Norman Morison,* along with Thomas Skinner, who had been hired to manage the farm adjacent to McKenzie's, his family, and 24 other families. They all had high hopes, but in truth they had absolutely no idea what awaited them on Vancouver Island or how quickly their hopes would be crushed.

On a cold and stormy day in January 1853, after a harrowing and hazardous five-month voyage from England, the *Norman Morison* anchored in Esquimalt Harbour. The fort was totally unprepared for such a large number of arrivals. The McKenzie party, expecting a warm reception and a comfortable home, was met instead by an HBC store clerk and herded higgledy-piggledy into an unpartitioned loft at the fort.

Disgusted with this treatment, and learning that the land they'd been hired to farm had, in fact, not yet been broken, McKenzie threatened to load his family and furniture back onto the *Norman Morison* and set sail for home. Anxious not to lose PSAC's newest and most promising recruit, Chief Factor James Douglas begged him to wait. He had horses saddled and took McKenzie and his party along the trail from the fort to the acreage that had been set aside for

It was not all work at Craigflower. This early 1860s photo shows the McKenzie family and guests setting off for a picnic. Craigflower Manor is in the background.

them. One glimpse of the breathtaking scene at the end of the trail, looking out over Portage Inlet, and they agreed to stay.

McKenzie named his farm Craigflower, after the Scottish estate of HBC governor Andrew Colvile. Its boundaries stretched from the Gorge and Portage Inlet to Esquimalt Harbour, from Thetis Cove to Skinner's Cove, where the Esquimalt Graving Dock is now, and bordered Skinner's Constance Cove Farm on its route back to the Gorge. Establishing his family in a log cabin on the property, McKenzie and his men worked hard to clear the land and make the farm productive.

Craigflower was a far cry from the relative civilization of the settlers' homeland, and many were homesick in those early years. Craigflower worker James Deans wrote: "So much did I feel the change and so homesick I became that I used to wander out in the bush and sit down, giving vent to my grief in a flood of tears."

Several men deserted for the California gold fields or turned to liquor for solace. But with better food and improved living conditions, life at Craigflower became more enjoyable, and within two years, 21 dwellings housed the 76-strong population. A sawmill, threshing

Patriarch Kenneth McKenzie, seated left, with sons (clockwise from left) Andrew, Robert, William, and Kenneth Jr. in the 1870s.

machine, kilns, brickyard, slaughterhouse, and a smithy supported the activities of Craigflower and surrounding farms.

In 1855 the colonists built a schoolhouse for the 30 children in the Maple Point neighbourhood, the waterfront land at the northwest end of Craigflower Farm. It was the first outside the fort and is still the oldest surviving schoolhouse west of the Great Lakes. By that time, Craigflower Farm had more than 1000 sheep, along with cows, working oxen, horses, pigs, and chickens. Its fields produced acre upon acre of wheat, turnips, and peas. The

farm's operations included a flour mill and a bakery that supplied the naval ships docking at Esquimalt Harbour with bread and biscuits. McKenzie's 630 acres were expanded to 900 acres of farming and grazing land, and on a gentle rise overlooking the Gorge waterway, a newer, grander home for the McKenzie family started to take shape.

By May 1, 1856, Craigflower Manor was ready for occupancy. An imposing Georgian Colonial structure, it had a heavy, iron-nail-studded front door and wooden shutters built into the walls, ready to slide into place to defend

Agnes McKenzie (seated left) and her daughters (clockwise from left)
Dorothea, Jessie, Wilhelmina Ann (known as Goodie), and Agnes.

against Indian attack. In fact, no such attack ever took place. The local Native people were friendly. Agnes McKenzie, whose servant girls had long since found local suitors and left the farm, hired Native women, who proved to be hard workers, reliable, and much taken by the white children in their care. All eight McKenzie children spoke Chinook, the West Coast trading language, fluently.

Like the Skinners and the Langfords, the McKenzies were lavish entertainers. Craigflower Manor, tastefully furnished in a style reminiscent of the McKenzies' Scottish home, soon became a social centre for HBC and naval officers, who delighted in the company of the McKenzies and

their lively young daughters. James Douglas and Dr. J.S. Helmcken, who described McKenzie as a "whole-souled gentleman," were frequent visitors.

Craigflower was an idyllic setting for the McKenzie children. Accustomed to the more restrictive atmosphere of their nursery in Scotland, they ran and played with abandon in Craigflower's rural surroundings. Life for the adults was equally free and fun-filled. Tea parties, riding parties, fishing, hunting, bathing, boating, croquet, and quoits were punctuated with constant comings and goings between the farmhouse and the fort, by boat along the Gorge or by horseback over the winding trails.

This panoramic view of Craigflower Farm shows the imposing manor on the slope behind the bridge, overlooking the farm outbuildings and the schoolhouse (at right).

Kenneth McKenzie never dabbled in politics, but he did become a justice of the peace and was appointed bailiff in charge of all four PSAC farms. Alas, his business success never matched his social success. Despite its early promise and the bailiff's best efforts, Craigflower and the other PSAC farms failed to meet the demands placed upon them. Unable to adequately service the fort and the visiting naval ships, McKenzie eventually had to import wheat from Oregon to augment his own supply.

Poor management, shortage of labour, and high wages doubtless played a part, as did the coarse, clay based soil—and the workers' well-documented battle with the bottle. Robert Melrose, a McKenzie worker and painstaking diarist, recorded the degree of drunkenness of each man, including himself, and how often each man was unable to work as a result. There were few days when all hands were gainfully employed.

Kenneth McKenzie left Craigflower in 1865 and settled with his family on his own farm at Lake Hill. In 1874 a fall from his carriage aggravated McKenzie's heart disease, and he died, aged 63, at home. Sir James Douglas and Roderick Finlayson were among the pallbearers at his funeral. He, his wife Agnes, and other

When he left Craigflower in 1865, Kenneth McKenzie and his family settled on Lakehill Farm. This view of the farm was taken looking east from present-day Douglas Street north of McKenzie in the 1890s, fifteen years after McKenzie's death.

family members are buried at Ross Bay Cemetery.

Over the ensuing decades, Craigflower Manor became a roadhouse for weary travellers bound for the Western Communities, an HBC employees' recreation centre, a summer camp for girls, and a museum. In 1956 it was declared an historic site, and in 1967 a government-funded restoration program allowed it to be opened to the public.

A visit to Craigflower Manor today, at a busy crossroads in the middle of a bustling suburb, is a brief but beautiful trip back into Victoria's past. Gone are the 900 acres of rolling farmland. But inside you can almost see the beautiful clothes, taste the tea, and hear the giggles of the children as they polished the banister with their sliding bodies.

Craigflower Manor stands as a testament to Kenneth McKenzie's early pioneering efforts. Just south of Christmas Hill, near the farm where he died, McKenzie Avenue and Kenneth Street perpetuate his name.

Where the top brass stayed

Today, Admirals Road is the southbound continuation of McKenzie Avenue, crossing the Gorge, passing through the Songhees Indian Reserve, and ending just north of Saxe Point. A hundred or more years ago it was a simple trail leading from Kenneth McKenzie's Craigflower Farm to the place where he once built a house for the most important local personage in the Royal Navy.

Victoria's development as a naval base began in the late 1840s. The Royal Navy's Pacific Squadron, operating out of Valparaiso, Chile, since 1837, needed a northern base for supplying and repairing vessels and for hospital facilities. Several sites were considered. Esquimalt was chosen. Between 1844 and 1846, Esquimalt Harbour was explored by Captain John Duntze on the frigate HMS *Fisgard* and charted by Lieutenant-Commander James Wood on HMS *Pandora*. It was Wood who named the islands and points around the harbour after Duntze and his men.

Admittedly, Esquimalt had its disadvantages. For seamen tempted to desert, it was distractingly close to the western United States, and it was far away from the Navy's patrol area in the South Pacific. But its advantages—a sheltered harbour, healthy climate, ready access to timber, provisions, and coal—were undeniable. A naval presence in the area had been welcomed by Chief Factor James Douglas, who presumed—correctly—that it would serve to prevent attack by hostile Natives. By 1865 an Order-in-Council of the British government authorized creation of a naval establishment.

In the early days, travel between Esquimalt and Fort Victoria involved a sea journey that was often made perilous by huge floating kelp beds. In 1852, sailors from HMS *Thetis* hacked a route eastwards, up and over Esquimalt Hill (Old Esquimalt Road), so that naval men and settlers arriving at Esquimalt Harbour could travel over a rough, three-mile trail through the forest to their new home.

Naval activity at Esquimalt increased with the outbreak of the Crimean War in 1854. Men who had been badly wounded in the ill-fated British and French attack on the Russian port of Petropavlosk had to be transported all the way to San Francisco for treatment. In 1855, with a second attack planned, Rear-Admiral William Henry Bruce, commander-in-chief of the Pacific Station, asked James Douglas to provide a temporary hospital. He responded by ordering the construction of three wooden hospital huts on Duntze Head. In fact, the

This 1862 painting by R.F. Britten shows some of the Royal Navy fleet at anchor in Esquimalt Harbour.

Russians deserted Petropavlosk. There was no attack and no wounded. The hospital huts housed only one patient—a sailor with scurvy. They were later used for theatrical productions.

When he arrived in Esquimalt in 1853, Kenneth McKenzie wasted no time in fostering friendships with Navy personnel. Like Thomas Skinner, who managed the PSAC farm east of Craigflower, McKenzie found the naval men good company and steady spenders. Before long the two—both fathers of several daughters— were supplying the Navy ships with provisions and the Navy men with pretty young social companions. Naval personnel also provided a much-needed link with home, enabling settlers to send and receive news and keeping alive the memories of a more genteel lifestyle.

Thinking to make the most of his naval connections, McKenzie built a comfortable home, which he called "Maplebank," near the southwest corner of his property, on the north shore of Constance Cove. His plan was simple: he would add to his farm's profits by renting the house to successive Navy admirals.

"Maplebank"—called "Admiral's House" while admirals and their families were living there—was surrounded by ancient maples. The house, grounds, paddocks, and stables were enclosed within a white picket fence. Lawns and gardens sloped down to a small beach. It was the perfect setting for garden parties and croquet games. The trail down from Craigflower was widened, to facilitate the passage of laden wagons and prominent partygoers, and was called Admiral's Road.

The first tenants of "Maplebank" were Rear-Admiral the Hon. Joseph Denman, FRS, Commander-in-Chief of the Pacific Station

"Maplebank," the admiral's residence, as it looked in 1870, just after Rear-Admiral Hastings' tenure ended.

from 1864 to 1866. Rear-Admiral the Hon. George Fowler Hastings, CB, and his family lived there from 1866 to 1869. Both men would later be remembered in city streets.

When McKenzie lost his position as bailiff of Craigflower, he tried to sell "Maplebank" to the Admiralty, but negotiations fell through. Eventually the house was taken over by the HBC. It burned down in 1910, the same year the Royal Canadian Navy took over the base.

Meanwhile, not far from "Maplebank," the buildings that in 1922 would form HMCS Naden had started to take shape. Originally the site of barracks built on Skinner's Cove to house Royal Engineers, it was taken over by the Royal Navy in 1862. The ten acres of land that surrounded the barracks became the site of the new hospital.

At the start of World War II, Naden expanded to become the principal Naval Training Centre for Western Canada In 1966, HMCS Naden became Canadian Forces Base Esquimalt. Today, it is primarily a barracks and instructional site. A summer tour of the museum and dockyard includes a look at present-day Admiral's House, built in 1885.

Kenneth McKenzie would not recognize the Admirals Road that nudges past Naden, crosses Esquimalt Road, and makes a straight run for the sea. On a sunny day the Strait of Juan de Fuca sparkles over the rooftops as you round the bend at the bottom—and then you're at Saxe Point, where the peaceful panoramic view is little changed from when the *Fisgard* and *Pandora* first sailed here, more than 150 years ago.

Where the Blinkhorns farmed

Tucked into the middle of Metchosin, just west of the golf course, Bilston Place is one of many cul-de-sacs leading off a winding street that connects Metchosin and Happy Valley roads. Back in the 1850s, however, this area was serene and unspoiled, fertile ground for an energetic farmer called Thomas Blinkhorn.

Blinkhorn (sometimes called Blenkhorn) was an Englishman, born and bred in Huntingdonshire. At the age of 31 he travelled to Australia. For 22 years he was engaged in stock-raising there and left his mark when he helped rescue Captain Sir John Franklin from almost certain death when he became lost in the bush. Lady Franklin never forgot this incident in her husband's career and was later to call on Mrs. Blinkhorn during a visit to Victoria.

Returning to England in 1849, Blinkhorn was contacted by James Cooper, a sea captain, who fired his friend Blinkhorn's imagination with tales of the new colony on Vancouver Island. When Cooper asked Blinkhorn to take charge of the farm he hoped to establish there, Blinkhorn readily agreed. Late in 1850 he set sail on the *Tory* with his new wife Anne, her niece Martha, Cooper, and the Langfords, who were to manage a farm in Esquimalt.

Martha Cheney was a bright girl in her teens, filled with a spirit of adventure, and a firm favourite among the *Tory*'s other passengers during the long and often stormy voyage. When she wasn't socializing, Martha kept a detailed diary. It is this diary—the only one written by a Vancouver Island woman of that period that has so far come to light—which tells us so much about this remarkable family and their life as independent settlers in their new Metchosin home.

Metchosin in those days was still very much as James Douglas had described it in 1842. No matter that its name derived from the long-ago rotting carcass of a dead whale (the Indian name "Smets-shosin" means "place of the stinking fish" or "place smelling of fish oil"). Douglas thought Metchosin "a very pretty place... There is, however, no harbour and the anchorage is exposed...on the whole it would not do for us." He settled on Camosack for the site of the Hudson's Bay Company fort, but he never forgot "the beautiful slopes, the richly tinted foliage... the bright clear sky" of Metchosin. Some years later he purchased land west of Cooper's and built a summer residence.

In 1851, however, the Blinkhorns and Martha were the first white settlers in the area. The three shared a log farmhouse on Happy

At Bilston Farm, the Blinkhorns welcomed many a weary traveller.
Their niece, Martha Cheney, was married in this house.

Valley Road near Bilston Creek, which had been named by Cooper after his birthplace in England. The farm's 385 acres stretched from the corner of Rocky Point and Happy Valley roads to the first bend up on Pears Road, then down Pears and across Metchosin Road to the edge of Witty's Lagoon near the waterfall. (Cooper built himself a cottage at Thetis Lake and travelled back and forth between the cottage and Britain.)

The warm and welcoming Bilston Farmhouse bulged with company. Captain W.C. Grant often overnighted on his way to and from his property in Sooke. The Langfords and the Skinners once walked there through snow, rain, and hail all the way from Esquimalt. Visiting friends from the Blinkhorns' *Tory* days regularly talked long into the night and fortified themselves with a huge

farm breakfast before facing the five-hour, fifteen-mile journey back to the fort.

Robert Staines, the fort's chaplain, had started a pig farm in Metchosin, and he and Thomas Blinkhorn became friends. In the summer of 1851, Blinkhorn, Staines, Cooper, and eleven other independent settlers signed a petition challenging the perceived tyranny of Chief Factor Douglas. This was the petition that ex-governor Richard Blanshard took with him when he returned to England after establishing a legislative council in an attempt to dilute Douglas's power. On March 29, 1853, that same council appointed Captain Langford (Esquimalt District), Thomas Skinner and Kenneth McKenzie (Peninsula), and Thomas Blinkhorn (Metchosin) magistrates and justices of the peace. The men in these positions

Captain Henry Bailey Ella

Captain Henry Ella, Martha Cheney Ella, and one of their children.

were the official local focus for law and order, charged with keeping the peace, settling disputes, and acting as middlemen between the settlers and Douglas.

Under Blinkhorn's energetic management, Bilston Farm continued to flourish. It was a strenuous but satisfying life. Anne Blinkhorn's niece Martha grew into a lovely young woman who could churn butter and help with chores all day, then dance on one of the naval ships till four in the morning.

Martha was still a teenager when Henry Bailey Ella came into her life. Henry, a Londoner, had gone to sea at the age of fourteen. As chief officer of the HBC barque *Norman Morison,* he regularly sailed between Victoria and England and first appeared in Martha's diary in January 1855. He must have made a good impression, for in July the two were married by the Reverend Edward Cridge at Bilston Farm.

Days of preparation had produced a sumptuous spread. There was no road to Metchosin, so the Langfords, Coopers, Helmckens, Douglases, and friends from the *Tory* rode out to Metchosin along the trails or paddled out by canoe in their wedding finery. It was a truly splendid affair and should have been the beginning of a long and happy life at Bilston Farm.

Alas, it was not to be. Little more than a year after the wedding the high-energy, hard-working Thomas Blinkhorn died. He was buried in the Old Burying Ground at Quadra Street. "I trust he has gone to rest, poor Uncle," wrote Martha in her diary.

The farm and its stock were auctioned off, and Martha, Henry, and Anne moved into Victoria to live on property owned by Mrs. Blinkhorn near the corner of what

Anne Blinkhorn

Wentworth Villa afforded a clear view west in the direction of the town and south across meadows and moorland toward Beacon Hill and the sea. It was a wonderful place to raise a family—plenty of oak trees for the children to climb, and an orchard and dairy—and "Grandmama" was more than welcome. The Ellas' seven children loved to gather round and listen to her tales of the *Tory* and the Metchosin farm and dances at the fort or aboard one of the many naval ships.

In 1873 tragedy struck. Captain Ella was drowned at Vancouver while attempting to cross Burrard Inlet in a canoe. Less than a year later, Elizabeth, the Ellas' oldest daughter, died at the age of seventeen. Ten years later, in August 1884, Mrs. Blinkhorn died of dysentery just three weeks after celebrating her 80th birthday surrounded by her family and friends at Wentworth Villa. The *Colonist*, which had so recently recorded the memorable birthday gathering, said, "Mrs. Blinkhorn has crowned a useful life with a beautiful old age."

The house saw its share of weddings over the years as the Ella children married and Martha became "Grandmama" to a new generation. Always ready to help others less fortunate than herself, she was known for her charitable works, and when she died in April 1911 the *Colonist* pointed out, "Her name will long be remembered in many homes throughout the city." The Ellas and Mrs. Blinkhorn are buried at Ross Bay.

Wentworth Villa still stands today at 1156 Fort Street—as solid and hardwearing as the pioneers who lived in it—and out in Metchosin, Mount Blinkhorn and Blinkhorn Lake are lasting reminders of the first white family who farmed in that "very pretty place."

is now the intersection at Broad and Yates, where several cottages formed the sum total of the houses outside the fort. Before long Mrs. Blinkhorn presented one of the cottages to her friend Reverend Cridge, for use as a hospital. It was the first hospital in Victoria.

By 1862 the town was growing by leaps and bounds, and the Blinkhorn property was sold to make way for more modern buildings. Martha and Henry Ella had already built a home on Cadboro Bay Road, as Fort Street east of Linden was then called, and Anne Blinkhorn joined them there.

Led to the Muirs

Some fifteen miles west of the farm at Bilston Creek is a stretch of road that used to be called Muir Avenue, after the Scottish family that settled there in the early 1850s.

The Hudson's Bay Company hired John Muir in 1849 to oversee a mining operation on the northern coast of Vancouver Island. The Muirs sailed from London's East India Dock on the *Harpooner*, a small, three-masted, merchant ship chartered to transport tradesmen and supplies to Fort Victoria. John and his wife Ann were accompanied by their widowed daughter Marion and her two young boys, their own four sons—Andrew, John Jr., Robert, and Michael—and their nephew Archibald. Also on board were John McGregor and his family, and the labourers hired by Captain W.C. Grant, who was travelling separately. John Muir had no way of knowing that the absent Captain Grant would one day figure largely in his family's future.

The *Harpooner* left London on December 1, 1848, came within sight of Vancouver Island on May 28, 1849, and landed at Fort Victoria on June 1. The Muirs and McGregors stayed at the fort until the end of August, when they boarded the *Mary Dare* bound for Fort Rupert, just south of present-day Port McNeill. It took them almost a month to reach their destination.

Sixteen Indian war canoes arrived at the harbour near Fort Rupert at the same time as the *Mary Dare*. The Kwakiutl men had just returned from battle and carried the heads of their enemies with them. Seeing Mrs. Muir—the first white woman of their experience—they politely offered her any two heads of her choice. To their surprise, she declined.

Fort Rupert was being constructed by a group of 40-odd workmen under the command of Captain William McNeill. John Muir Sr., John Work of Fort Simpson, and John McGregor set off by canoe to look for the best place to mine coal. One month later Muir and his sons and McGregor started to sink a pit.

But all was not well. The local Natives were warlike and threatening, which made the mine workers uneasy, especially since they worked some distance from the fort and were unprotected. Equally vulnerable were their families, alone at the fort while their men worked. Some of the miners demanded to be allowed to remain above ground to protect their wives and children, but HBC co-operation was not forthcoming. Tempers flared and work at the mine stopped. The men were ordered to dig drains. Arguing that they had been hired as miners, not labourers, they refused. The new colony's first strike was under way.

John and Annie Muir

Despite the best efforts of Dr. J.S. Helmcken, who had been appointed justice of the peace by Governor Blanshard, the troubles were not resolved. When their HBC contracts ended, Andrew Muir, John Muir Jr., and most of the McGregors departed for San Francisco and better fortunes. They would soon return. In the meantime, John Muir Sr. took what remained of his family back to Victoria and bought land at Sooke.

In 1852, when coal was discovered at Nanaimo, Governor Douglas sent John Muir to oversee the operation. But his heart wasn't in mining any more, and he returned to Sooke. This time he stayed, and he bought a parcel of land adjoining his own—the farm that had

belonged to the soon-to-depart Captain Grant, who had decided to return to England.

United as a family once again, the Muirs poured their energies into their property, Woodside. They were hard workers and used to a simpler life than the decidedly upper-class Grant, and soon houses, outhouses, storehouses, and mills adorned their property. Their steam-powered sawmill just west of Whiffin Spit produced lumber for export to San Francisco and Hawaii.

There still was no road to Sooke. In 1852 Governor Douglas had had a rough trail constructed from Fort Victoria, but it was not wide enough for wheeled wagons and carriages. In 1855, when Martha Cheney and Henry Ella were married at Metchosin, the Muirs dressed in their Sunday best and made the fifteen-mile journey by horseback.

By 1860, when John Muir Sr. was elected to the legislative assembly as member for Sooke, the trail was still only passable for horses and cattle, which may have been part of the reason why he missed many meetings. Butter, turnips, and potatoes from Woodside Farm reached Victoria in large canoes paddled by Indians.

The lack of suitable access was a huge deterrent to settlers. A few did move onto the land they had bought nearby, but through the

The Muirs established a sawmill, farm, sailing fleet, and logging operation on their property, which is now part of Sooke. By 1869, when this photo was taken, the sawmill was in full swing.

1860s the Muirs were the most firmly established and undeniably the most successful. Business, in fact, was booming, thanks to their logging operation based at Muir Creek, which ran down from the west side of Muir Mountain to the waterfront west of Otter Point.

They built a small fleet of sailing vessels, one of which—the clipper *Ann Taylor*—helped carry their lumber to distant ports that now included London, Australia, China, and Japan. They acquired more land, eventually owning most of present-day Sooke. And they built a classic, Georgian-style farmhouse in place of their original single-storey home.

Despite the flurry of activity that surrounded the 1864 discovery of gold at Leech River, the Sooke area remained virtually inaccessible by road until the 1870s. By then the trail from Victoria, little changed since its construction in 1852, was often blocked with fallen trees. The steamer *Sir James Douglas*, which brought mail and passengers from Victoria, only sailed once a month, and when it was laid up for repairs, communications came to a grinding halt.

The powers that be finally decided to build a proper carriage road to Sooke, and Muir won the contract to construct a bridge over the Sooke River and a road to Woodside Farm. The bridge was opened in 1872. That same year a log-cabin schoolhouse was built on Muir's land, near present-day Sooke and Caldwell roads. The post office established during the Leech River gold rush, then closed, was reopened at Woodside with Michael Muir as postmaster. It wasn't until 1887, however, that the road was extended from Jordan River Road, as Otter Point Road was called in those days, right to Woodside's gates.

Early in 1875, Annie Muir died. She had been a favourite with the local Indians, and during her last illness they had often called at the house with small gifts. She was the first person laid to rest in the part of the Muir property that had been set aside for a burying ground—the Muir Cemetery on today's Maple Avenue.

John Muir and his sons continued to operate their mill—now larger and relocated closer to where today's government wharf stands at the foot of Maple Avenue—until it was destroyed by fire one early summer morning just a few months after Annie's death. The fire had

already taken hold by the time they reached the mill. It quickly spread to the well-stocked granaries, and the Muirs stood by helplessly as twenty years of hard work disappeared before their eyes. There was no insurance.

Dismayed but undaunted, the Muirs built another mill, which they later moved to a new site on Sooke Harbour. Sadly, their heyday was over. They soon began to feel the strain of competition from mills at Port Alberni and Burrard Inlet.

John Muir Sr. died in 1883 and was buried beside his wife in the Muir Cemetery. Years later, the road he'd waited so long to see became just another section of Sooke Road. But their house still stands, south of where Grant Road meets West Coast Road, and in the memories of the descendants of this region's earliest and most enterprising pioneers, Muir Avenue lives on.

"Woodside," the 3,360-square-foot farmhouse that replaced the Muirs' original one-storey home, stands to this day on Sooke Road, west of the town centre.

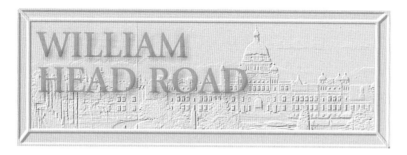

Who was William Head?

Where did he come from? Why is there a road named after him? And how was he related to Albert?

No prizes for guessing that there was no such person as William Head. The headland at the south end of Parry Bay was named for Sir William E. Parry, a famous British Arctic navigator and explorer. Parry Road and Parry Cross Road, which run east from William Head Road toward Parry Bay, are also named after him. Albert—who bore no relationship whatsoever to William—was HRH Prince Albert of Saxe-Coburg and Gotha, husband of the queen for whom our city was named.

Albert Head, at the north end of Parry Bay, was the site of the area's first Dominion Government Quarantine Station, where people coming into the country by sea would stop to be examined for communicable diseases. Anyone carrying such a disease stayed at the station till it ran its course. The station was built in 1883, but within ten years it was replaced by a larger facility at William Head, some four miles south.

The William Head station, staffed by thirteen families and with its own school and chapel, was a stopping-point for ships of all sizes, from square-riggers to junks and ocean liners. It

was also a mustering point for people. During World War I, 80,000 Chinese were held at the station on their way to and from France, where they formed labour battalions, working behind the lines.

Advances in medical treatments eventually made the quarantine station redundant. It closed in 1958 and reopened as a federal minimum-security prison. Now it is the William Head Institution, a federal medium-security penitentiary, and the road running north from it—known as Quarantine Road from the 1920s to 1961—is William Head Road once again.

Between Albert Head and William Head, Parry Bay stretches in an unbroken line, affording a magnificent view of the Olympic Mountains. This was—and still is—the "very pretty place" described by James Douglas, and more than a hundred years ago, four very different families farmed here.

Witty's Beach Road reminds us of a Loyalist who came to these shores during the San Juan Islands dispute. In 1867 John and Charlotte Witty bought land that had once belonged to James Cooper's Bilston Farm, where the Blinkhorns

The site of the William Head Quarantine Station, shown here in November 1917, is now the location for William Head Institution, a federal minimum-security penitentiary.

Built with money donated by subscribers including Sir James Douglas, and on land donated by John Witty, the Church of St. Mary the Virgin is the third oldest Anglican church in continuous use on Vancouver Island.

had settled fifteen years before. It was a beautiful piece of property with a sunny, east-facing aspect, an abundance of fresh water, and a good-sized chunk of waterfront including a lagoon. There were other families in the area that might be glad of John Witty's expertise as a blacksmith. And the price—$6000 for 385 acres—was right.

Over the next few years the Witty family grew from six to ten, though a one-year-old baby drowned, and a son was later lost while sealing in the Bering Sea.

In 1871 John Witty donated two acres of land for a school, church, and churchyard. Sir James Douglas headed the list of subscribers to the Building Fund with a donation of $100. Two of John Witty's children were among the ten who, in 1872, attended Metchosin school's first class. Church services were held in the schoolhouse until the Church of St. Mary the Virgin was completed the following year.

Witty didn't live to see the church's consecration. He died one day before the ceremony as the result of a knee injury sustained while shoeing a horse. His funeral service was the first held in the church, and he was buried in the ground he had given. Thirty years later he was joined by Charlotte, who died of tuberculosis at the age of 58. Their farm is long gone, but their descendants live in the area to this day.

Today you can drive to the end of Witty's Beach Road, pull into the parking lot, and take a footpath to the 86 stairs that lead down to Witty's Beach, a favourite summer picnic spot and almost as tranquil as when the Wittys first moved here, more than 130 years ago.

Mary Ann and George Pears

East of Witty's property, Pears Road commemorates George Pears. Born at Eton, in Buckinghamshire, England, Pears stopped briefly in Victoria in 1862 on his way to seek gold in the Cariboo. Returning after six months, he took up dairy farming at Beacon Hill before moving to Metchosin around 1867.

In 1871 he married Mary Ann McMeakin, who had come to Metchosin via Ireland and Liverpool, England. Pears built a log cabin on Witty's property, and the couple lived high on the cliff overlooking Witty's Beach until repeated Indian raids persuaded them to move farther inland.

In the year he married, George Pears built Metchosin School on the land donated by John Witty. The cost was $300, half of which was covered by the settlers and half by the government. The school, which started off with one teacher, was added to as the years went by and today serves as the museum where Metchosin's early history is preserved.

Mary Ann died in 1907 at the age of 58. George stayed at Crofter's Farm, selling out and retiring about six months before his death at the age of 74, in 1913. They are buried together in St. Mary's Churchyard.

Nine of the couple's twelve children lived, and many of their descendants survive to this day— living reminders of the Pears of Pears Road.

⌒ ⌒ ⌒ ⌒

Duke Road, which leaves Metchosin Road, then rejoins it after cutting across the western end of Albert Head, is named after a family that arrived here in 1884. Thomas Duke was born in London, England, and had gone to Ontario as a boy. He and his wife Ann were teachers who yearned for a different life on Canada's West Coast.

Thomas Duke

They travelled by train to Portland, Oregon, and thence to Victoria by boat with four-year-old Alfred and three-month-old Annie. They bought land on Albert Head Road (now Duke Road), where teacher-turned-farmer Thomas cleared more than 50 acres. Before long he was selling dairy products, meat, eggs, and fruit to buyers in Victoria.

Ann Duke was a brave woman. One evening while returning from Victoria, she became lost as darkness fell. Ann walked around her horse team all night to keep warm, then guided the team home at sunrise.

Like mother, like daughter. Little Annie was only seven years old the day she was sent to fetch help for her sick mother. On her four-mile walk through the woods, Annie came across a huge cougar. It crouched on a fallen log beside the trail. She stared at it. Hard. The cougar stared back, then slowly turned and slunk away.

Besides being brave, Annie was also very good at elocution and essay writing and once won a life-size portrait of Queen Victoria in a district-wide school competition. Even getting to school was an achievement. Sometimes Thomas ferried the children across the channel at Witty's Lagoon, but most days they made the six-mile round trip to Metchosin School on foot. The Dukes later sold land to the school board for a school at Albert Head.

Thomas Duke was 65 when he died in 1905. Alfred developed diabetes and died at the age of 28, 13 years before insulin was discovered in the province of his birth.

Annie married John Trotter, who died in 1915. She stayed on the farm with her mother and her children for another ten years before moving in to Victoria. Ann Duke died in 1941 at the age of 102. Annie was 84 when she died in 1969. The Dukes are buried together in St. Mary's churchyard. Duke Road passes the old farm and farmhouse, which is still standing.

⌒ ⌒ ⌒ ⌒

Leefield Road, between Happy Valley and Kangaroo roads, is named for a Kansas farmer

*Edward and Phoebe Field
on their wedding day in 1873.*

who travelled with his young family to Metchosin in 1877.

Edward Spellman Field, his wife Phoebe and their year-old son, Chester, settled on land that comprised a small clearing with a few log buildings, small farmhouse, barn, blacksmith shop, and combination chicken- and root-house. A trail ran through to Happy Valley Road. The farm was enlarged under Crown grants, and eventually 100 acres were cleared using manual labour and draft-horse power.

A second son, Lee, was born in 1882. When he got to be school age, one of his close friends at Metchosin School was Annie Duke. The Fields had been the first to welcome the Dukes when they arrived from Ontario in 1884, and in fact seven-year-old Annie's encounter with the cougar took place en route to the Fields' home. As the Field boys grew up, they took over most of the farm work, coming home along the winding, dirt road after school to carry on with ploughing or carpentry repair work.

In the late 1800s the Fields turned their efforts to logging and built a water-powered sawmill on Bilston Creek. Their lumber was used to build Metchosin's first phone-box in 1908 and a new home for themselves in 1912. But they later returned to farming as well, and by 1900 their 500 acres backed onto Kangaroo Road and adjoined property that contained most of Blinkhorn Lake and Mountain. Edward Field died in 1917, at the age of 74. Phoebe Field died October 1941. They had remained close friends with the Dukes, whose tombstones lie beside their own in St. Mary's churchyard.

Next time you take a summer picnic up to Tower Point and gaze across Parry Bay toward William Head, remember the men, women and children who were among the first to call this place home.

The first Royal Oak hotel

What do Chatham Road and Royal Oak have in common? A man named Richard Cheeseman.

Cheeseman was born in 1823 in Chatham, Kent, England. In 1849 he signed on with the Hudson's Bay Company, and in 1850 he came out to Fort Victoria as a fur trader or factor. He sailed from England on the *Norman Morison* with almost 80 other immigrants, including the young doctor J.S. Helmcken.

The HBC had allowed him to buy five acres of land stretching eastward from just north of the fort out to Spring Ridge. A rough road ran through the property, and Cheeseman built himself a log cabin beside it. He named the road Chatham, after his hometown in England. Coincidentally, many years later, Chatham Road in the same area would commemorate a vessel commanded by Lieutenant-Commander Broughton in 1792.

Like Helmcken, Cheeseman was transferred for a few months to Fort Rupert, where he traded with the Indians. Before and after this posting he made several trips on horseback to the Lake district (today's Royal Oak), travelling north to Elk Lake, then west to Prospect Lake—trading as he went and looking for a spot to settle and raise a family.

In May 1851 Cheeseman went back to England, and in early 1852 he married his Sevenoaks sweetheart, Jane Dyke. They returned to Vancouver Island together on the *Norman Morison,* along with the Skinners and the McKenzies, who were coming to manage PSAC's Esquimalt-area farms.

Jane Cheeseman Durrance

The barque's chief officer was Captain Henry Bailey Ella, who two years later would marry a pretty young lady in Metchosin. This wasn't his first such assignment, but it surely was one of the roughest. With a length of 119 feet, a width of 26 feet, and a depth of 20 feet, the 529-ton vessel wasn't built for comfort. Three decks and a poop deck were barely sufficient for the 80-plus passengers and crew, and inclement weather kept the ladies down below for most of the five-month voyage.

Jane Cheeseman and Mary Skinner were pioneer wives who shared a special bond   both

There was much socializing between the Saanich pioneers. Here the Thomsons, Durrances, Duvals, and Goyettes are pictured together. In the back row, left to right, are: William Thomson, Johnny Durrance, unknown, John Durrance, Janie Cheeseman Duval, Jane Cheeseman Durrance, Louis Duval, Ethel Duval, Mr. Goyette, Mrs. Goyette with baby, and Margaret Thomson. And in the front are W. Duval, H. Goyette, and two unknown children.

In April the Cheesemans loaded their belongings onto an open wagon and set out for the Lake district. Over the years, Cheeseman had developed a good trading relationship with the local Natives, and now they proudly escorted him to his new home.

It took them four days to make the five-mile journey along the winding trail through wolf, bear, and panther territory. At night they pitched a tent. By day they moved ever farther from the fort. For Jane, used to more civilized surroundings and with a four-month-old babe in arms, it must have been a terrifying journey.

The Indians led Cheeseman to the best location for a dwelling on the land he had purchased—the Colquitz River,

were expecting babies. Mary Skinner's sixth child would eventually greet the world in a humble shack not far from Fort Victoria. Jane's first child—a daughter named Mary—was born as the *Norman Morison* was hurled around Cape Horn in the middle of a hurricane.

The Cheesemans arrived at Esquimalt in January 1853 and spent four months at Fort Victoria. Intent now upon a different kind of life, Richard searched for and found the perfect place to raise a family. He asked the HBC to release him from his duties and exchanged his downtown property for 214 undeveloped acres in the wilderness, five miles north of the fort.

a little way south of its origins at Beaver Lake. The Cheesemans lived in their tent while, with the Indians' help, they cleared land and built a log cabin. They called their access trail Cheeseman Lane.

In 1854 they started to clear land for their future family residence and the area's first hotel. It was built near where the trail forked—the beginnings of West and East Saanich roads. Walking on the property with her daughter Mary one hot summer day, Jane paused for a while in the cool shelter of a particularly large tree. Looking up into its dense foliage, she remarked to Mary, "This truly is a *royal* oak!"

The second Royal Oak Hotel was built by Louis Duval across the street from the site of the original building, which burned down in 1887. Duval had bought the first hotel from Jane Cheeseman Durrance, who was soon to become his mother-in-law.

And so the hotel, and eventually the surrounding area, was named.

With a hard-working husband and a healthy, growing family, Jane must have felt truly blessed. But fate was soon to deal her the first of many blows. In 1862 Richard was killed in a freak accident when his horses bolted down Cheeseman Lane. He was laid to rest in the Old Burying Ground on Quadra Street.

Suddenly widowed, with four children under the age of ten to care for, Jane nevertheless saw the hotel building and the area's first post office to completion. But life was hard for a young woman alone. Two years later she married James Bailey, of Rose Hill Farm, and another daughter was born.

In 1864 Jane Cheeseman Bailey donated land beside the hotel for the Lake district's first school, which was to serve as school, community hall, and church. Built by James Bailey and other volunteers under the supervision of Mr. Van Allman, the school opened in 1865 with fifteen pupils. It was destroyed by fire in 1883. Two years later, Royal Oak School was opened and stands as a Heritage Building to this day.

Jane suffered another loss in 1871. Bailey died of a heart attack in January, and she was left a widow once more. In April she married John Durrance and moved to his Spring Valley Farm on Durrance Road. Their son, John, was born in 1872.

Louis Duval, who arrived at Royal Oak that same year via Quebec and the Cariboo, bought the Royal Oak Hotel and Post Office from the Cheeseman Durrance family in 1873. By 1875

Richard Maynard took this photo of the Durrances' Spring Valley Farm, in the 1880s, ten years after Jane married John Durrance.

he was living there with his new wife, Janie Cheeseman, third daughter of Jane and the late Richard. When the hotel burned down some twelve years later, Duval built a second hotel across the street (East Saanich Road), which opened for business in 1890.

Four years earlier, Duval had given land for St. Michael and All Angels Church on West Saanich Road. Now he helped build it, clearing land, hauling lumber, and hand-cutting all the shingles for the roof. The church was dedicated on St. Michael's Day, 1883, and Duval's third son, Fred, was the first child christened in it. Among Duval's many other contracts was the laying of Sooke Road out from Colwood Corners. In 1887 the road was extended as far as Otter Point, where it joined up with John Muir's road to Woodside Farm.

On August 20, 1897, Jane Cheeseman Bailey Durrance died at the age of 66 and was buried at St. Stephen's Anglican Church. Finding her grave isn't easy. On the stone, her last name is spelled Durance, her first name is given as Mary, and there is an incorrect date of death.

Her descendants have done their best to set the record straight. Thanks to their untiring efforts, the Cheeseman family's seven generations are commemorated—correctly—on the walls of the library at Commonwealth Pool, which was built on Cheeseman property. Go take a look sometime. It's a fitting tribute to the brave pioneers who put the "royal" in Royal Oak.

McPhail settled there first

Who was the Newton of Mount Newton Cross Road? Some say it was the bookkeeper for Captain Langford of Colwood Farm, a Newton who married John Tod's daughter Emmaline. Others say it was a man who assisted surveyor-general Joseph Pemberton; the latter held this Newton in high regard and may well have immortalized him with a namesake mountain. But one thing is certain—by the time the first survey stake was driven into the summit of Mount Newton in 1858, several pioneer families were well and truly established in the area, including Angus McPhail's, William Thomson's, and Duncan Lidgate's—the three who settled there first.

Angus McPhail (or McPhale, as Pemberton wrote on the original land deeds) will go down in history as South Saanich's first white settler. He was a Scot from the Isle of Lewis who signed on with the Hudson's Bay Company in May 1837. Sailing on the *Prince Rupert* from Stromness to York Factory the next month, McPhail spent a year in the Red River District. Then he was transferred to the Columbia Department and served at Fort Langley. While there he married a Cree woman, who died while giving birth to his daughter, Anne.

In 1846 McPhail was transferred to Fort Victoria. He operated a dairy southeast of the fort, not far from the foot of present-day Blanshard Street, and furnished a steady supply of milk and butter for most of the next decade.

McPhail married again in June 1851, to a woman reputed to be his first wife's sister. In 1855, having made a name for himself as an efficient, productive herdsman, he left the HBC and the hustle and bustle of the fort and moved his family north into the area called Sanitch, or Saanich as it's known today.

In February 1852 the Indians had surrendered, "entirely and forever," the areas called North and South Saanich to James Douglas, agent for the HBC. There is no official record of the total price paid, but three conditions of sale were: the Native people could continue to live in places where they were already encamped; they could continue to hunt and fish; and there would be a proper survey of the land. The Mount Newton area was provisionally surveyed soon after the purchase, but it was still virtually undisturbed three years later, when Angus McPhail arrived.

McPhail staked out 170 acres on Saanich Inlet, near the western end of Mount Newton—land that would be officially allotted to him when John Trutch completed the HBC survey

A sketch of Angus McPhail's cabin.

for Pemberton in 1858. It would be another eight years before Mount Newton Cross Road was built, and the winding horse-trail (eventually West Saanich Road) leading up from the Cheesemans' place at Royal Oak didn't permit wagons to pass.

Supplies for Bay Farm had to be floated around the peninsula by sea—a journey of four days from Fort Victoria to the cove just west of McPhail's place. He didn't consider it an inconvenience. This, he had concluded, was the best place to build a home and the perfect place for a farm. Fewer trees covered Mount Newton's gentle lower slopes, the soil in the hollow below was rich and fertile, the ground was well irrigated by water, and it was peaceful. His only neighbours were the Natives on the reservation to the south and the wild animals that roamed

the densely wooded hillside to the north.

An energetic axeman and builder, McPhail felled trees, hand-hewed and grooved squared logs, and cut shingles for his 20- by 30-foot cabin. It was here that Marie, his second daughter, was born in 1859, just before McPhail received pre-emption papers for his property. As a married man he was allowed to pre-empt up to 200 acres (single men were only allowed 100), so took rightful ownership of all the land he'd staked out four years before.

Nobody knows what prompted his next move, but in 1860 McPhail sold part of his property to Peter Lind, who would soon build the area's first hotel. In 1862 he sold the rest of Bay Farm to Alphonse Verdier, who had recently married sixteen-year-old Anne McPhail. Less than a year later, Anne's stepmother died.

George Stelly moved to Saanich in 1869, buying a farm at the west end of today's Stelly's Cross Road. Angus McPhail may have worked for George, and McPhail's son-in-law eventually bought Stelly's farm.

Widowed for the second time, McPhail left the area and apparently worked in Cowichan, where it is reported his younger daughter was cared for by the Sisters of St. Ann, a nursing and teaching order of nuns that came to Victoria in the early 1850s.

In those pre-Malahat Drive days, the only access to the western side of Saanich Inlet was by water. Some years earlier, when Thomas and Mary Skinner of Constance Cove Farm had decided to look at land in Cowichan, they had to follow a winding trail some fifteen miles to McPhail's place and on to Thomson's Cove, where Indian canoes were waiting. The Skinners made the round trip across the inlet, then stayed at Bay Farm overnight before travelling back to Victoria.

When he moved back to Saanich in the early 1870s, McPhail apparently worked with George Stelly, whose farm would also eventually be purchased by McPhail's son-in-law. In 1875 his second daughter, Marie, married Frank Gravelle, son of a former HBC man.

McPhail's whereabouts during the next few years are unknown, but it is reported that he ended his days at the Old Men's Home in Victoria, situated conveniently, but perhaps with little thought for the implications, on the northwest corner of Ross Bay Cemetery.

McPhail died at St. Joseph's Hospital in March 1884, at the age of 75. He was buried, with George Stelly's son as sole mourner, in the cemetery's Roman Catholic section, close to the water. In 1911, when Dallas Road and the Ross Bay sea wall were constructed, his grave was relocated to higher ground.

So ends the story of Angus McPhail. Bay Farm is no longer—Woodwyn Farm now stands on the property—but McPhail Road bears witness to his presence here. He is remembered by descendants and by the Saanich Pioneers' Society, whose log-cabin museum contains fascinating relics, records, and reminders of those early Mount Newton days.

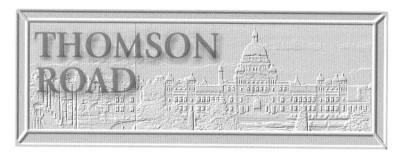

Second Mount Newton settler

*J*ust a short distance east of Angus McPhail's place, near the junction of West Saanich and Mount Newton Cross Road, you will find Thomson Road and Thomson Place, named after McPhail's neighbour, William Thomson.

Thomson was born in 1829 on a farm in Forfarshire, Scotland. A shipwright by trade, he signed on at nineteen as ship's carpenter on a freighter carrying supplies to the army fighting in the Crimea. Eventually, like many others, he succumbed to the lure of the California gold rush and sailed to San Francisco. He worked at the port there, caulking vessels against the rigours of the sea.

Before long, wanderlust struck again, and in 1854 he boarded the *William* bound for Vancouver Island. Disaster struck on New Year's Eve, when the storm-tossed ship ran onto rocks near Clo-oose, at the mouth of Nitinat Lake. As it broke up and sank, Thomson and fifteen other crew members managed to reach the shore, where they were met by a group of Native people and taken back to their village.

There were no overland routes in those days, and traditionally the Natives did not attempt to paddle their huge canoes down the coast during the stormy winter months. Stranded on the west coast until the weather improved, Thomson and his shipmates worked in the village. In the spring, when the Natives took their pelts to Fort Victoria, they took the white men too—and traded them to Governor Douglas.

Not thrilled at having to pay for men he hadn't expected in the first place, Douglas supplied them with clothing and goods and put them to work. Thomson was sent to Cadboro Bay to help build an HBC barn on a farm there, and later he worked at Craigflower. At some point he met the Lidgates and a herdsman by the name of McPhail, his future neighbours. Like McPhail, Thomson had had enough of working for the HBC, preferring to take his chances in the undeveloped wilderness of Saanich. McPhail moved up to Mount Newton in June 1855; Thomson arrived a month later. He called his farm Bannockburn, perhaps because this part of Saanich reminded him of a place in Scotland, site of a long-ago battle in which the Scots defeated the English.

The two men built cabins about a mile apart. The first livestock for Thomson's farm—nineteen pigs—arrived by boat in the bay at the west end of present-day Mount Newton Cross Road several days after they left the fort and seemed none the worse for their journey. It was a good beginning.

In December 1856, William Thomson and Margaret Dyer, step-daughter of his Craigflower co-worker Duncan Lidgate, were married at Victoria District Church by Reverend Cridge. For a time they lived on the lower part of Yates Street, and their son David was born there the next year. Six months later, when Thomson was ready to take his wife up to Mount Newton, Margaret was pregnant again.

For the seventeen-year-old mother, with a baby strapped to her back, the hours-long journey on horseback along the narrow, winding trails over Little Saanich Mountain must have seemed endless—and ultim-ately disappointing. Margaret couldn't contemplate staying in the primitive cabin Thomson had built, so he took her back to Victoria and quickly con-structed a four-room timber home higher up the slopes.

When he brought her back a second time, the Thomsons were here to stay. In March 1859 their second son, Alexander (Alec), was the first white child born in the area. Between 1857 and 1882 the Thomsons had ten sons and five daughters. Two sons died in childhood accidents, and two more sons would die before the age of 40.

Twenty years younger than his neighbour McPhail, Thomson was a man of boundless energy and enthusiasm who set a pattern of work and diligence that became a Saanich trademark. Over the years, as his family increased in size, he enlarged his home more than once. As well as farming, he built and maintained many roads on the peninsula and in the Cowichan area.

William Thomson

Active in local affairs from the start, he joined other pioneers in creating a close-knit community. In 1862 he gave land for, and helped build, an Anglican Church (St. Stephen's), although he was a staunch Presbyterian. There were no sawmills in the area, so California redwood timbers were shipped around to what is now Thomson Cove and hauled by oxen to the site of the future church.

Concerned about the lack of formal education for his own and other neighbourhood children, Thomson agreed to sell four acres of land to the government for the area's first schoolhouse and then helped build it on the slopes of what is now Raven Hill Farm. The school was later moved to East Saanich Road. Thomson served as school trustee until 1895.

He was one of the instigators of the Saanich Agricultural Society and served as its president many times over the years. The first Saanich Fair was held in 1869 on McTavish Road. The second and third fairs were held at Bannockburn. Absolutely everybody came to the fair, some travelling around the peninsula by sea from Victoria because the overland journey took too long.

The Thomsons were noted for their hos-pitality and offered many a traveller a place to stay en route to Victoria. Weddings were commonplace and their annual New Year's parties were legendary.

Life on a Saanich farm was not without its hardships. Like others around him, Thomson suffered during one or two particularly difficult

William Thomson donated the land where St. Stephen's Anglican Church still stands. The two tiny Christmas trees he planted on either side of the porch now tower over a building that is little changed since it was consecrated in 1862.

winters, when thick snow blanketed the area. Once he lost a whole flock of HBC sheep that were wintering on his property, and he almost lost his best horses when the roof of his large stable caved in under the weight of the snow.

Despite these and other setbacks over the years, Thomson did well. Toward the end of the 1880s fellow North and South Saanich farmers and their sons joined the Thomson men in a barn-raising of the best kind. Reported to be the largest structure of its type on Vancouver Island, the barn was made of Thomson's own timber, felled and prepared mostly by himself and Alec, his second son.

By the time William Thomson died in August 1908, the wild land he'd helped pioneer was not too far north of a bustling city with a busy Inner Harbour that boasted magnificent Parliament Buildings and the recently opened Empress Hotel. When Margaret Thomson died in October 1920, Victoria was experiencing the depression that followed the elation at the end of the Great War.

William and Margaret are buried together in St. Stephen's Churchyard, in the area they loved so well and contributed to in such great measure. They live on in the minds and hearts of the many descendants who remain on the peninsula to this day.

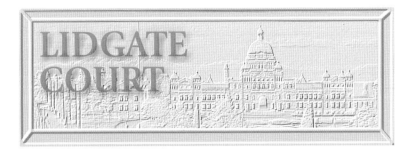

The last of the first

Considering that the Lidgates lived on Mount Newton Cross Road, it seems strange that Lidgate Court should be several kilometres farther south. There's a simple explanation. When the Saanich municipality realized that one of its earliest pioneers was not currently recognized, it named a small street off the north end of Helmcken Road in his honour. Was it just a coincidence that Lidgate and Dr. J.S. Helmcken sailed here on the same ship, three years apart?

The Lidgates' story begins in Haddington-shire, Scotland, where Duncan and Helen, both widowed with young children, married and started a family of their own. In 1852 Duncan Lidgate signed on as a carpenter with the Puget's Sound Agricultural Company and set sail for Fort Victoria.

The *Norman Morison* was on its third trip to the new colony. In 1850 it had brought Dr. Helmcken, the Cheesemans, and others to these shores. In 1853, when the Lidgates made the long voyage round Cape Horn, the passenger list included two PSAC farm managers including Kenneth McKenzie, Duncan Lidgate's new boss.

Like most of the men who laboured for McKenzie, Lidgate found him a difficult employer, but he worked the next five years at Craigflower as required by his agreement. One of his projects was to help build Craigflower School—the first in the area—and his children became pupils there in 1855.

By 1858, Lidgate had served his time and was happy to leave Craigflower behind. Allotted

William and Margaret Lidgate

The Lidgates' Rose May Cottage, built in 1858 and much renovated, stands to this day.

25 acres as part of his HBC agreement, he had originally taken up land at Four Mile House. Now he chose farmland east of William Thomson's place in the Mount Newton area, about halfway between the two trails from Fort Victoria that climbed up the west and east sides of the peninsula.

Lidgate had met William Thomson at Craigflower and helped him build his first Mount Newton home. Present-day Thomson Road marked the point where the Thomsons' land ended and the Lidgates' began, but the family ties were so strong that the fence was a mere formality. Thomson was now Lidgate's son-in-law, having married his step-daughter Margaret in 1856, and the Lidgates were already proud grandparents of two small boys.

In those days there were no roads. It would be another six years before the pick-axes and shovels of the pioneer road-builders created a route—Mount Newton Cross Road—that connected West Saanich and East Saanich roads and extended to Saanichton Bay. The trails running north from Fort Victoria were crossed only by a west-east trail south of Hagan Creek that connected the Indian reserves on either side of the peninsula. There were two routes to Victoria: over Little Saanich Mountain on horseback along a tortuous trail, or around the peninsula by sea from the waterfront at Saanich Inlet. Both journeys could take several days to complete.

Happy enough in their somewhat isolated surroundings, Mount Newton's first settlers set about creating a new life for themselves. House-building was a community effort. White men and Natives worked side by side, clearing land, constructing houses, raising barns. Putting his carpentering skills to good use, Lidgate built a fine home, which he called Rose May Cottage. Before long his farm had livestock and was producing wheat and fruit.

Helen was a welcome addition to the community and always much in demand. She was a competent nurse and midwife. Many children of those early Mount Newton pioneers were guided gently into this world by "Granny Lidgate's" capable hands.

The Thomsons and the Lidgates enjoyed cordial relationships with the Natives. As a young girl at Craigflower, Helen's daughter Margaret had formed a friendship with the daughter of the chief of the Tsartlip village, a friendship that was renewed when the Thomsons and Lidgates settled just north of the Tsartlip Reserve. Margaret conversed with the Native women in Chinook, the lingua franca of the Northwest coast, developed by the Natives for trading and picked up by the fur traders and HBC men when they arrived in the area.

In the early 1860s Lidgate helped William Thomson and others build St. Stephen's Church, and served as church warden. He also helped organize the Saanich Agricultural Society and participated in its many functions.

Duncan Lidgate died in 1874, at the age of 60, and was buried at St. Stephen's. Ten years later, Helen married another Saanich man, Edward Pritchard. In 1888, after a long and fruitful life, she died at the age of 74 and was laid to rest beside Duncan in the family plot, close to the door of the church her husband helped build.

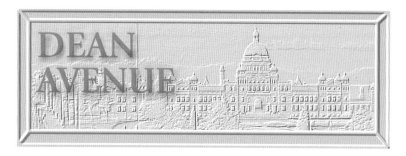

DEAN AVENUE

"This splendid country"

Running parallel to Richmond and Foul Bay, Dean Avenue starts at Fort and stops at Lansdowne, just like the man it's named after. George Deans (a clerical error omitted the "s" when the street was named) was a Scottish labourer who worked at Fort Victoria before settling on a farm in Saanich.

Deans was one of eighteen men hired by Kenneth McKenzie to work on Craigflower Farm in Esquimalt. With his wife Ann and brother James, Deans sailed from England on the *Norman Morison* in August 1852.

The passengers had much in common. Like Duncan Lidgate and two others, Geordie Deans was a carpenter from Haddingtonshire, ready to try his luck in a new land. Like Jane Cheeseman and Mary Skinner, Annie Deans was expecting a child. She delivered her first—a daughter named Mary—not long after the ship reached its destination.

Confined to her bed for almost all of the gruelling five-month voyage, Annie was thankful for their safe arrival at "Royal Bay." The first of many wonderful letters from her new home described the anchorage—"a splendid bay about half a mile from the shore of Vancouver's Island"—in glowing terms. Equally colourful was her description of the men who paddled

out to greet them on that cold January day. They were, she reported with amazement, "almost naked—nothing on them but a red or blue blanket."

Deans, his wife, and 38 others went out to Craigflower with McKenzie. But it wasn't long before 22-year-old Geordie was at odds with his autocratic employer. One day in April 1853, he and Duncan Lidgate were reported "absent with complaint to Mr. Douglas about food."

Shortly after, Deans and another carpenter left Craigflower and went to work for Thomas Blinkhorn on James Cooper's property out at Metchosin. Furious, McKenzie had the two men apprehended and imprisoned for a month in the bastion. Both refused to return to Craigflower and served out their contracts with the HBC instead, based at the fort.

The work was plentiful and the money was good. One year after his arrival, Deans bought a town lot near the fort. Writing home with the good news, Annie explained why her last letter had gone astray—it had been sent in care of Fort Victoria's chaplain, Reverend Robert Staines, who had perished when his ship foundered off Cape Flattery. She also advised her relatives that letters would reach them faster if they were addressed "via New York, to George Deans,

Carpenter, Victoria, Vancouver's Island, North West America." A year later she wrote again, worried that there were still problems with the Russians up north and reporting that three hospital buildings had been erected west of the fort "for the sick and wounded of the English fleet."

Geordie, steadily employed in the construction of Victoria District Church and the parsonage that would house the fort's new chaplain, Reverend Cridge, bought more land. Annie helped out by doing

Geordie and Annie Deans

sewing for the wives of HBC men. By 1858, when Geordie was released from the HBC, they were the proud owners of 112 acres in Victoria district, 200 acres in the Lake district—and two more children. Ellen was a bright, healthy girl, but Alec died suddenly of a cholera-like illness when he was eighteen months old, soon after they had moved to their farm.

"Sunnybrae" (later renamed "Oakvalle"), which was also the name of their Victoria district farm, stood on the southeast corner of the Mount Tolmie and Deans Cross Road intersection (now the intersection of Richmond and Lansdowne). Today it's a busy thoroughfare. In the late 1850s the area was totally isolated, crossed only by two rough trails. One, later to become Cedar Hill Road, was the Indian route from Cedar Hill (later Mount Douglas) to Fort Victoria. The other, eventually Cedar Hill Cross Road, was

formed by the feet of the animals and men who travelled between North Dairy Farm at Lake Hill and Uplands Farm at Cadboro Bay.

Annie, devastated by the loss of her son and missing adult female companionship, entreated her brother and sister in Scotland to move out to "this splendid country," promising "you will make more in a day here than what you would earn at home for a fortnight." Apparently they weren't to be persuaded.

A second son, George, was born in 1859, and a daughter, Anne, in 1861. James, who had been working as a shepherd for McKenzie at the HBC's Lake Hill Sheep Station on Christmas Hill, joined his brother and sister-in-law on their Saanich property on completion of his PSAC contract.

In 1868, sadness struck the Deans family. Fifteen-year-old Mary, the "stout, bonnie little lass" born soon after their arrival in 1853, died during a diphtheria outbreak. She was buried in the Quadra Street Cemetery.

Two more children—Katie and John—rounded out the family, but in 1879 tragedy struck again. Geordie was attempting to catch a horse in the corral. It turned and kicked him full in the pit of the stomach. His injuries were fatal; within fifteen minutes Geordie, 48, was dead.

Annie lived on at "Oakvalle" with her six surviving children for another eleven years. In

The Deans' farm sat at the intersection of Mount Tolmie (Richmond) and Deans Cross Road (Lansdowne). Grafton Tyler Brown painted the property in the 1880s, looking south towards the Strait of Juan de Fuca.

1890 she died of Bright's disease, an inflammatory disorder of the kidneys.

James, meanwhile, had made quite a name for himself as a geologist, ethnologist, anthropologist, linguist, and poet. An intrepid traveller, he studied the Natives of the Northwest Coast and in 1892 he prepared an exhibit, including a model of an entire Haida village, for the World's Fair in Chicago. He died in 1905, aged 78, having outlived his brother by some 26 years.

Geordie and Annie Deans are buried together at Ross Bay under a magnificent monument that bears witness to the passing of this pioneering pair.

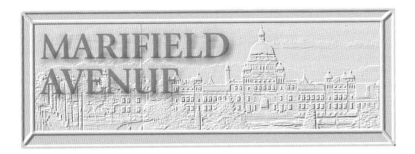

Home of the Cridges

To be or not to be? That might be the question posed by a small street in James Bay, which ends (rather abruptly) at a fence—as though it started out to be a street, then changed its mind. Yet within its short, uncertain length, Marifield Avenue holds memories of a powerfully positive pioneer—Bishop Edward Cridge.

Born in Devonshire, England, in 1817, Edward Cridge was a schoolmaster before earning a BA at Cambridge. He was ordained at the age of 31, in 1848, and was working in London when he saw the London newspaper ad that was to change his life. The Hudson's Bay Company, it seemed, was looking for a chaplain to replace Reverend Robert Staines, who had been lost at sea. Cridge didn't hesitate. Gathering up his new bride and his treasured cello, he set sail on the *Marquis of Bute*. Five months later the ship anchored off Macaulay Point. It was April 1, 1855.

The Cridges settled in quickly—the large, light rooms of Fort Victoria's barn-like accommodations must have seemed like heaven after almost half a year cooped up in the ship's small cabin—and the new chaplain was warmly welcomed. His predecessor had been quite a character, but of late had rather neglected his duties as chaplain in favour of his pig-farming activities. Wasting no time, Reverend Cridge immediately started religious services in the fort, while Mary Cridge operated the Sunday School.

They established themselves in James Bay, as it was called in those days, on the west side of what is now Government Street. "Marifield" boasted a beautiful garden and an orchard, a henhouse, woodshed, and barn, Victoria's first tennis court, and a fresh-water well. Marifield Avenue led to the family home.

"Marifield" was a wonderful setting in which to raise children, but the Cridges' four offspring, aged ten months to just under three years, all died of "black measles" during two months of the 1864-65 winter. They were buried in the Quadra Street Cemetery. Of the five children born subsequently, only three survived into their parents' old age.

Cridge quickly discovered that his chaplaincy extended far beyond the fort's four walls. As more and more settlers moved to outlying areas, he travelled by canoe or on horseback to communities in Esquimalt, Colwood, Sooke, Metchosin, Royal Oak, Mount Newton, and Nanaimo, baptizing, marrying, and burying, holding services in people's homes until churches could be built.

Victoria District Church, also called Christ Church Cathedral, stood atop Church Hill (now Burdett Avenue). It burned down in 1869 and was replaced by a larger wooden structure.

Cridge's contributions to the new colony were numerous and far-reaching. In 1856 he read the opening prayers at the first session of the legislature. Shortly after, Governor Douglas appointed him acting inspector of schools, an unpaid post that he held for nine years. His efforts to improve the lot of the unfortunate were legendary. After a sick man was deposited on his doorstep one morning in 1858, Cridge helped Dr. Helmcken and others establish the settlement's first hospital. It was for men only, based in a cottage at the corner of Yates and Broad streets that had been donated rent-free

by his friend Mrs. Blinkhorn. Later he helped found the Female Infirmary at the eastern end of Pandora Avenue, at its intersection with Chambers Street. The two were later combined as the Royal Hospital. Meanwhile, Mary helped found the Protestant Orphans Home in 1873 (renamed the Cridge Centre for the Family over 100 years later).

In 1856 the Victoria District Church, also called Christ Church Cathedral, was built on the site where the Law Courts sit today, the first cathedral in British Columbia. When Bishop George Hills arrived in Victoria from England

During almost six decades in Victoria, most spent at "Marifield," Bishop Cridge (inset portrait painted by Teresa Pemberton) saw the town grow from a small HBC community to a bustling provincial capital.

in 1860, he made Reverend Cridge first dean of the cathedral. That first wooden church burned down in 1869, and a second was built on the same site, also of wood.

In April 1858, parishioners coming down the church steps in the warm spring sunshine after morning service heard a great commotion from the harbour. The first wave of Fraser River-bound gold miners had arrived, and the Hudson's Bay Company settlement would never be the same again. Victoria had always been a male-dominated environment, but now men outnumbered women by 100 to one. The situation was temporarily alleviated by the arrival in 1862 of a boatload of single women—sent by the Emigration Society in England at Cridge's request—but twenty years later young adult men still outnumbered young adult women three to one, and the city had become a hotbed of bawdy behaviour.

During the 1870s, however, Cridge had other, more pressing concerns. His relationship with Bishop George Hills, sweet enough to begin with, had turned horribly sour. The two did not agree on the tone of church services— Hills apparently favoured more ritual, while Cridge opted for less—and Cridge found it more and more difficult to accept Hills as his superior. The dispute

The Reformed Episcopal Church of Our Lord, consecrated in 1876, was built with the donations and labour of its own congregation.

In 1877, Sir James Douglas's funeral service was conducted at the little church he had helped found at the bottom of the hill below Christ Church Cathedral.

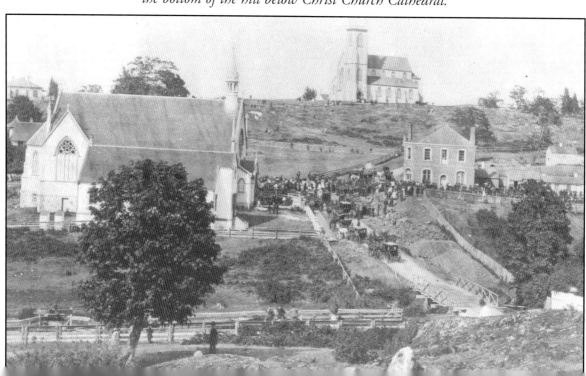

became rancorous. Eventually Cridge was brought up in church court and found guilty of insubordination to the bishop. It was the beginning of the end.

Cridge left the Church of England. In a heart-warming display of loyalty, half of his congregation followed him, trooping down Church Hill to the east end of the James Bay mudflats at Humboldt Street, where a new place of worship quickly began to take shape. Sir James Douglas donated land for the building and found an organ to furnish it. He and Dr. J.S. Helmcken, both staunch Cridge supporters along with most of the HBC old-timers, committed themselves to this new enterprise. It was truly a community effort, as evidenced to this day in the little white structure constructed of Douglas fir, with its interior finished in California redwood, where windows, communion table, reading desk, lectern, pulpit, altar rail, choir pews, and belfry chimes commemorate those early supporters.

The first service in the Church of our Lord was held in January 1876, and the congregation voted to join the Reformed Episcopal Church. Cridge was made a bishop. A year later Sir James Douglas was buried from this church, with Bishop Cridge officiating.

In 1898, 42 years after Cridge read the opening prayers for the first legislature, he performed the same honour at the legislature's first session in the new Parliament Buildings on Victoria's Inner Harbour. He preached his last sermon in 1908 and died at "Marifield" in 1913, eight years after his beloved wife. He was 96.

Today, highrises have replaced the tall oaks and maples that used to grace the Cridge property. Still, in James Bay's network of criss-crossing streets, meandering Marifield Avenue creates a welcome diversion and a permanent reminder of the beloved chaplain who once ministered to the pioneers of this place.

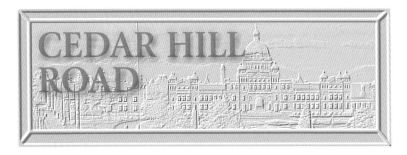

The first Gordon Head community

Next time you travel south on Cordova Bay Road, don't follow the curve that leads you onto Shelbourne—drive straight on, down Cedar Hill Road and back into history. For this was the route followed more than 150 years ago by up-Island tribes on their way to trade with the HBC men at Fort Victoria. Starting at the eastern end of Cordova Bay, they created a trail along the eastern side of Cedar Hill, as Mount Douglas was then called, following the hills and valleys south to the settlement on the Inner Harbour. It was at the northern end of this trail, where the Indians beached their canoes to avoid the dangerous riptides around Ten Mile Point, that Gordon Head's first settler laid claim to land. As you drive along the 4200 block of Cedar Hill Road, picture in your mind's eye the simple log hut on the hill built by James Tod, the first white man to call this area home.

James Tod was the son of HBC Chief Factor John Tod, whose career had spanned several decades and several HBC locations across the country. An early liaison in Manitoba with a woman called Catherine had produced a son, but John Tod had quickly abandoned James and his mother in favour of other, more interesting pursuits.

By the time James caught up with his father at Fort Vancouver in 1840, John was married to his fourth wife and seemed quite astounded that James, now a strapping young man in his early twenties, had turned out so well. "He is a great stout fellow," remarked John in a letter to a friend, "and a regular ploughman."

In 1850 James followed his father to Fort Victoria. John soon retired from HBC service and built a home in Oak Bay, while James began a career in farming that would last more than 50 years. He became familiar with HBC farms at Lake Hill and Cadboro Bay—establishments connected by the rough east-west trail that would later become Cedar Hill Cross Road. The area north of this trail, however, remained untouched until James, having worked in and around the fort for two years, decided to strike out on his own.

Like Geordie Deans and many other former HBC workers, he seemed intent on moving as far away from the fort as he could, and he chose a remote acreage at the top end of that north-south Indian trail. In the early 1850s, Gordon Head was no more than a rocky headland named after Captain the Hon. Charles Gordon, who visited this coast in 1845 to help define the British-U.S. boundary.

Captain Gordon didn't think much of the area that was to bear his name. In fact he went on record as saying he would not give one of the barren hills of Scotland for all he saw around him. Fortunately, many disagreed with him. James Tod was the first. In August 1852 he registered his claim with colonial surveyor J.D. Pemberton and became the proud owner of Lot 17.

The 260-acre section was long and narrow, stretching from the Government Reserve on Mount Douglas across the Mount Douglas Beach area almost to Duart Road, then running southward to Winchester Road—streets that in the 1850s were not even a twinkle in some road-builder's eye. Tod's claim was a mixture of thickly wooded land, oak-studded meadows, and several streams that continued to flow clear and free through the height of summer. Preparing the land for farming would be a challenge, but Tod—more than six feet tall and strong as an ox—wasn't daunted. It took five long years, but by October 1857 he had bought more land, built a log cabin high on a hill where he could be lord of all he surveyed, and was ready to bring home a bride.

Flora Macaulay was no stranger to pioneering life. Seven years earlier her father, Donald Macaulay, had brought his wife and four daughters to the southern tip of Vancouver Island when he was appointed bailiff of PSAC's Viewfield Farm in Esquimalt. Flora, now seventeen, was ready to start a new life. With

Flora Tod (left) and her eldest son Jim in the 1880s.

the blessings of Reverend Edward Cridge, Flora became the wife of James Tod—more than twenty years her senior but with the energy of a man half his age. Before the year was out, she would bear the first of her seventeen babies.

James's talents as a carpenter and wheelwright had proved useful as he built and furnished their log-cabin home. But there was still land to be cleared and trees to be felled and shaped into sheds, barns, and fences to protect the growing flock of sheep from the wolves, cougars, and racoons that considered this area their own.

The Tods were brave and hardy souls. Few young mothers today could tackle a cold and bitter winter like the one nineteen-year-old Flora faced with two young children, a new baby, and weather so cold that even the wolves took shelter under the small family home. Snow covered the ground for 90 days. James, away for most of that time, struggled to save his sheep when thousands on the peninsula around him were perishing.

Still, they succeeded. By the spring of 1869 James was able to build a "more commodious dwelling," just in time for the birth of his seventh child. Spring Farm was no longer so isolated. Others had cleared land and created homes along Cedar Hill Road. A school and a church had been built, and James and Flora's children attended both.

The Tods were strict parents—it was the only way to keep their growing brood under

Flora Tod and four of her seventeen children in the 1880s.
The boy to Flora's right is Tom, her youngest.

control. All the children had chores. The boys took turns climbing the crooked tree at the foot of today's Ash Hill, ready with a gun to protect their father's sheep from cougars. As they grew older, the boys helped run the farm and made trips to town to barter foodstuffs for cobbling or blacksmithing services.

Like other early settler groups, Gordon Head's pioneers helped each other with building, seeding, and harvesting. James Tod's steam threshing-machine was much in demand. It took six horses to pull the steam tractor, and the "Cock o' the North," three blasts of the steam whistle, heralded its arrival at yet another farm.

In the 1890s, James and Flora's eldest son, Jim, answered the call of the Klondike. By this time only four of the Tods' surviving offspring were still at home, and another would marry and leave within the year. Two sons and a baby daughter had died. Six years later another daughter was lost to "galloping consumption."

In 1898, Jim returned empty-handed from the North and resumed his duties as the eldest son. By this time Flora, worn out by motherhood, was being cared for in a sanatorium. Eventually the only Tods left at home were James, 44-year-old Jim, who was still a bachelor, and Tom, 17.

James, who had never been sick a day in his life, gradually started to weaken. His sons fed him and cared for him until one day in 1904, when Jim was away in town and Tom was out in the farmyard, James quietly breathed his last. He was 86 years old.

This view of farms in the Cedar Hill District was taken in the 1880s.

Like his children before him and his wife ten years after him, he was buried at St. Luke's, the wooden church at the junction of Cedar Hill Road and Cedar Hill Cross Road, where carefully engraved monuments on a large plot bear testament to this remarkable family's presence amongst us.

The day after James Tod purchased his second section (Number 52) on the southeast corner of today's Mount Douglas Park, a new neighbour moved in next door. On April 18, 1857, Robert Scott became the second Gordon Head landowner by purchasing two side-by-side sections farther south.

Scott's sections (53 and 54) formed an elongated triangle that started from Glendenning Road, ran east across the valley just north of Feltham as far as Gordon Head Road, headed slightly northwest along the line of Kenmore to James Tod's boundary at Columbia, then doglegged south to align with Winchester before continuing west back to Glendenning.

Today that pie-shaped wedge encompasses a school, a community centre, and a park. In 1857 there was nothing but the heavily wooded east slope of Cedar Hill, a neighbour to the north who had already cleared some of his stream-nourished land, and the wild animals that still freely roamed this area. But a veritable land boom was in progress. In two more years the entire 2200-odd acres of Gordon Head would be shared among thirteen men.

Little is known of Robert Scott's movements before he reached Gordon Head. It is believed, however, that he may have lived first in the Mount Newton area. Although land records proclaim Angus McPhail as the first white settler there, the area's first residents—the Native people—believe that someone else got there first: a fair-skinned man who spoke their language. A man by the name of "Bob." In fact, the record shows that Scott bought land close to the Tsartlip Indian village in 1855. He worked first for Captain Edward Langford at Colwood Farm and then with Robert Laing, a shipbuilder. Scott was one of the carpenters who, along with Laing and Geordie Deans, helped build Victoria's first Anglican church.

In 1857 he apparently moved to the Cedar Hill area, and just three weeks after James Tod and Flora Macaulay were married by Edward Cridge, Robert Scott and Robert Laing's daughter Elizabeth took their matrimonial vows in the same little wooden structure, high on Church Hill.

The two couples had much in common. Like Tod, Scott was several years older than his young bride and chose to build a home for her on a hilltop. With their Indian helpers, the men cleared land and planted crops, while their young wives kept house and trusted that their husbands wouldn't fall prey to the cougars and wolves that seemed reluctant to share this land with its human invaders. Before half a dozen years had gone by, each woman's pioneering spirit would be tested more than once, and each would bring three children into the world.

But there the similarities ended. Elizabeth's marriage came to an abrupt end with her husband's untimely death in 1864, at the age of 36. They

had been married only seven short years. St. Luke's Church and its churchyard were still to be built, so unlike other Gordon Head pioneers, Robert Scott lies buried at Quadra Street.

Left with three young children to care for, the young widow turned to John Spence. Formerly of the HBC, Spence was a remarkable man who took on the little family, marrying Elizabeth and becoming a second father to her three offspring. Elizabeth lived only a few more years. She died in October 1872, a few weeks after her own mother.

By this time, the north-south Indian trail that ran through the western section of the Scotts' property had been widened to form Cedar Hill Road. The Scotts shared the whole length of their southern boundary with Peter Merriman. Manager of James Douglas's Fairfield Farm before moving to Cedar Hill, Merriman built a house on the east side of Cedar Hill Road, a little south of present-day Torquay Drive.

The Scott children had many others their own age to play with—the Tods to the north, the Merrimans and the Irvines to the south— and were soon of an age to have families of their own. It wasn't to be.

Robert Junior, the oldest child, was a handsome man who worked hard and successfully on the family farm. Robert had a long-time lady love, the daughter of another pioneering family some distance away. He harnessed his four fine horses and visited her every Sunday. But each had other responsibilities—a bachelor brother in her case, a sister whose marriage had failed in his. Robert, engrossed in farming and political activities (he was a councillor for the municipality) didn't look elsewhere. He died in 1921, a wealthy man and a bachelor to the end.

An unidentified photographer took this photo of the Cedar Hill area from Mount Tolmie in the 1890s.

Isabelle Scott, the sister Robert felt responsible for, had married in her mid-twenties and separated from her husband, R.J. Hawkey, a few years later. She died in 1935.

Jane Ann's story was a sweeter one. Her marriage to George Davidson was by all accounts a good one. They shared an abiding interest in church activities, George preaching at Christian Endeavour meetings while Jane sang in the choir. It is said that, until the day he died, George wore a watch-chain braided from Jane Ann's hair.

By the mid-1930s all of Robert and Elizabeth Scott's children were gone, and as none of them had children of their own, the family lives on in name only—just one of those early settlers on Cedar Hill Road.

∽ ∽ ∽ ∽

Five years after James Tod started to clear section 17, and two days after Robert Scott laid claim to sections 53 and 54, the line of settlement along Cedar Hill Road crept farther south with John Irvine's purchase of section 41.

Irvine was a Hudson's Bay Company man who, like so many others, had struck out on his own as soon as he could. His acreage in Cedar Hill must have seemed like heaven after life on a PSAC farm.

Recruited in the Orkney Islands, Irvine, his wife Jessie, and their small family had set sail for Vancouver Island on the supply ship *Tory* in November 1850. They were in good company. One fellow passenger was former chief trader John Work, who would one day own land both west and east of the Irvines' Gordon Head home. Also on board were the Langfords, James Cooper, and the Blinkhorns.

John Irvine's Rose Bank Farm was close to Cedar Hill Road and its cross road. Here (left to right) Mary Ann Laing and her daughters, John and Jessie Irvine, Margaret Irvine, an unknown woman, Jim Tod, and Jack Irvine with his wife and children stand in a field beside the house and barn in 1892.

The six-month journey around the Horn on the 105-foot long, 25-foot wide *Tory* was deadly dull at times. Week after week, seabirds and porpoises provided the only signs of life, and there wasn't much opportunity for privacy for the passengers crammed on board.

When they arrived at the HBC post in May 1851, the *Tory*'s 100-plus immigrants nearly doubled its existing population. Soon after their arrival at the fort, the head count increased by one with the arrival of the Irvines' son, William.

Like most other early immigrants, William's parents were less than enchanted with the conditions that greeted them—not at all what they had been led to expect. The Irvines moved out to Craigflower where, true to his contract, John served

his time and saved his money. By April 1857 he was ready to leave Portage Inlet behind.

The land he purchased on Cedar Plains was a mixture of meadows and dense woodland. It stretched from just east of Braefoot Road across to Gordon Head Road, and from just south of McKenzie down to Mortimer. Eventually he would own land extending north of McKenzie almost to Laval—a total of 300 acres—but it was near the northern boundary of his first section that he built his home. Here, he and Jessie would raise their children, and here they would eventually end their days.

Enchanted by the profusion of wild roses everywhere, the Irvines called their farmhouse "Rose Bank." It was large, welcoming, perfect for a growing family—and of particular interest to a fellow by the name of Alexander Garrett.

Bishop George Hills had charged Reverend Garrett with the care of those who lived outside the city. It was a huge job. There were many groups to minister to, and the men who had finished their indentures with the HBC continued to move farther afield; the community at Cedar Hill seemed to grow almost daily.

Garrett needed a place to gather his flock. "Rose Bank," situated close to the intersection of Cedar Hill Road and its cross road, seemed heaven sent. No matter that its owners were Presbyterians; like William Thomson over at Mount Newton, the Irvines generously supported the Anglican Church's efforts to supply Christian services to pioneer settlers.

The first Sunday service at "Rose Bank" in 1860 attracted twelve adults and twelve children. Before long the congregation overflowed into the Irvines' barn. Clearly a separate building was needed, and in 1862 St. Luke's Chapel was built. Along with the Chapel came Church Farm, managed by Mr. and Mrs. Henry King.

It was Mrs. King who first attempted to educate the settlers' male children. Two hours a day in her own kitchen, armed with only her King James Bible, Mrs. King introduced George Deans, Jim Tod, Peter Merriman, and Jack Irvine to the alphabet. Later, studies continued in St. Luke's Chapel. Later still, a half-acre of donated land a little farther west provided space for a separate school and a master. This meant a longer walk to lessons—and more time for adventure—for the Irvine's second son, Jack.

Bright as a button and bursting with energy, Jack had a problem. He couldn't tell the time. He hid his difficulty by conferring with his friend Jim Tod when the need arose, but he was finally caught out. One day, as the result of mischief, he was told to stay behind after school—alone—for fifteen minutes. Without Jim to help, he apparently sat ... and sat ... and sat.

He may have had trouble figuring out which was the big hand and which was the little one, but there was certainly nothing wrong with his eyesight. "Long Gun Jack" grew up to be a crack shot, much respected by the Indians with whom he hunted. Years later, a nearby road was named in honour of his prowess with a rifle.

Meantime, his parents were growing older. Cared for by their unmarried daughter Margaret, they stayed at Rose Bank Farm until they died, John in 1906 and Jessie a year later. Both are buried at Ross Bay Cemetery.

Today, two schools stand on land that once belonged to the Irvines. Rose Bank Farm is long gone, but generation after generation of John and Jessie's descendants still cherish their pioneer roots.

In the built-up hustle and bustle of the area, it's hard to believe that the whole of present-day Gordon Head was once owned by thirteen men. On the north-south Indian trail that became Cedar Hill Road, James Tod, Robert Scott, and John Irvine numbered among the first.

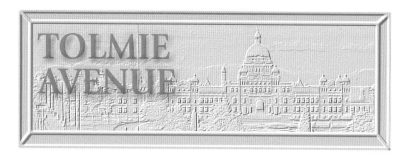

A man of many firsts

There's an interesting connection between "Long Gun Jack" Irvine, a huge tree on a quiet Saanich street, and a man by the name of Tolmie. Jack's parents owned property next to William Fraser Tolmie's huge estate. Tolmie donated land for the school attended by Jack and the other Cedar Hill children—and planted the seeds for that huge sequoia tree.

By the time he settled in Saanich, Tolmie had had a long, productive career. Born at Inverness, Scotland, in 1812, he graduated from medical school and by the age of twenty was bound for a new life in the Pacific Northwest. His voluminous journals record his adventures in colourful detail.

Sailing around Cape Horn on the *Ganymede* in 1832, he was probably the only one of the passengers who enjoyed the long, tedious voyage. For him, there were never enough hours in the day. A voracious reader, he busied himself with his studies, fishing, playing his flute, and attending to the myriad medical ills experienced by fellow passengers. He ended his eight-month journey at Fort Vancouver, ready to begin a career in the service of the HBC.

Almost ten years later he returned to Scotland, this time by a different route—across the Rocky Mountains on foot, then along the waterways to York Factory, on Hudson's Bay, and the ship that would take him home. It had occurred to him that it was time to think about marriage. "A wife," he confided in his journal, "is the only being to whom one could unreservedly pour out his soul." Perhaps he would find one in his homeland.

But it wasn't to be, and Tolmie returned to Fort Vancouver in the 1840s. On one of his frequent visits to Fort Victoria he renewed his acquaintance with the young woman who would put an end to his bachelorhood—Jane, eldest daughter of another HBC pioneer, John Work.

In 1850, when Tolmie was 38 and Jane in her early 20s, the two were married at the fort by the Reverend Robert Staines. Tolmie bought 100 acres of clover-covered land west and north of his father-in-law's property, then returned with Jane to Fort Vancouver.

Like all the brave young wives of HBC men in those times, Jane followed her husband into wild country, and like her mother before her, she strove to educate mixed-blood wives of fur traders and help them build better lives for themselves.

The first of their twelve children was born in primitive conditions, but in 1859 Tolmie was

The Tolmie family at "Cloverdale" in 1878. Jane Work Tolmie is in the middle row of seated people, at left, while William Fraser Tolmie is at the right end of the same row.

transferred back to Victoria to manage PSAC's Vancouver Island operations. He settled the family in a fifteen-room home that he called "Cloverdale." It was built of stone and California redwood and was surrounded by large oaks and firs along with a sequoia and the area's first Hawaiian acacia and Oregon ash trees, grown from seeds brought from Fort Nisqually.

"Firsts" were second nature to Tolmie. He was the first white man to attempt to climb Mount Rainier and the first practising physician and surgeon in what later became British Columbia. He was also the first to breed shorthorn beef cattle and the first to introduce

strawberry plants, dahlia seeds, and California quail to Vancouver Island.

He quickly developed many interests in his new community. He spearheaded the Victoria Agricultural Society and served as a member of the legislative assembly from 1860 to 1866, taking a special interest in road construction, postal communications, and the improvement of Indian health. He had seen the pressing need for free education as early as 1859 and spent many years fighting for this principle. The Deans, Tod, Merriman, and Irvine children were the first to benefit from his efforts. He was later appointed to Vancouver Island's first Board of Education

"Cloverdale," built of stone and California redwood, was surrounded by trees grown by Dr. Tolmie from seeds he brought from Fort Nisqually.

and helped develop the basic groundwork for our present educational system.

Becoming more and more engrossed in politics as the years went by, Tolmie supported B.C.'s entry into Confederation. He was an enthusiastic advocate for the transcontinental railway, favouring a route through the Yellowhead Pass that would connect the mainland to the Island with a railhead at Esquimalt. His deep-seated interest in public affairs was passed on to his youngest son, Simon Fraser Tolmie, who became premier of B.C. in 1928.

The Tolmies raised seven sons and five daughters at "Cloverdale." Ten were still living at the time of Jane's death in 1880. Tolmie himself—medical doctor, musician, botanist, explorer, agriculturist, and legislator—died in December 1886, aged 75. He and Jane are buried together at Ross Bay Cemetery.

Tolmie and Cloverdale avenues, Mount Tolmie, and the many streets named after Scottish places and persons remind us of this remarkable man. And at the south end of a Lovat Avenue apartment building, which stands today where "Cloverdale" stood for more than a hundred years, that huge sequoia tree shelters the memory of his name.

Grand street for a man with grand ideas

At the end of a long finger of land attached to the southwestern tip of the Tolmie property lay the inland waterway James Douglas once called the "canal of Camosack." And immediately west of Tolmie's land was the property owned by one of Douglas's most outspoken critics—James Yates.

James Yates was a shipwright, born in Scotland in 1819 and trained at the Dysart shipyards. Twenty-nine years later he signed on with the Hudson's Bay Company.

James and Mary Powell Yates had been married only two short weeks when they set sail from London on the merchant ship *Harpooner*. They made an interesting twosome. Where James was tall, temperamental, and stubborn—Dr. J.S. Helmcken would later describe him as "a powerful cantankerous being"— Mary was small, gentle, soothing, and a firm favourite with all the children on board.

It was a wild voyage, made even wilder by the antics of the mischief-loving sons of John

An old glass-plate photo of James and Mary Yates

Muir, hired to work at a mining operation on the northern coast of Vancouver Island. The midwinter weather at Cape Horn did its worst. Churning seas, howling gales, and hailstorms battered the little ship. Calmer weather up the coast provided a welcome respite, and at the end of May 1849 the *Harpooner* nosed cautiously through the narrow opening into the harbour and deposited its passengers near their new home.

One look at Fort Victoria's sparse and uncomfortable accommodations was enough to persuade the voyagers they would be better off back on their ship. Roderick Finlayson, the HBC man in charge of the fort, made no attempt to welcome them or to apologize. He was not, after all, responsible for the misleading advertising that had lured his new charges to this place. Nor was he particularly sympathetic to their plight; in his twelve years with the Company he had known far more primitive surroundings than these.

Not long after the *Harpooner* docked, James Douglas arrived to take charge of the fort. He was met by a group that was most vocal in its protests concerning the living conditions. Douglas promised to pass on the settlers' complaints, but as far as James Yates was concerned, it was too late. He was not impressed with his new boss and did not hesitate to say so.

Yates wasn't the first to fall foul of James Douglas, nor would he be the last. After eighteen long months as an HBC employee, he could stand it no longer and assumed independent status. It was a smart move. His new business was about as far removed from carpentering as could be and proved a great deal more lucrative. Yates became a wine and spirit merchant, proud owner of the settlement's first watering hole, the Ship Inn on Wharf Street, just north of the fort.

This did nothing to endear him to Douglas, but most others in town supported the entrepreneur's efforts—at least in private. By the time the Company was ready to sell town lots, Yates was in the position to buy two and

established his family in a home outside the fort.

Business at the Ship Inn was brisk, and before long Yates was able to expand his land interests. In 1852 he purchased almost 400 acres along the north side of the Gorge waterway. His eastern boundary was later shared with Dr. Tolmie who, because land was subdivided at different times by different people, eventually owned a narrow strip extending from his Cloverdale property through to the waterway.

Yates's Craigie Lea Farm boasted horses, oxen, cattle, pigs, sheep, and chickens and was soon producing grain, root vegetables, and butter. It was a perfect setting for a growing family—Emma, Harriet, Mary, and baby James—and Yates decided to move them into the country, away from Wharf Street's noise and busyness.

The wide street he had built east from the Inner Harbour now extended beyond Government. When prospectors en route to the Fraser River swarmed into the settlement in the

Lower Yates Street in the 1860s was a wide thoroughfare lined with wooden hotels, saloons, and other businesses.

James Yates's Ship Inn was on Wharf Street between Heaney's Cartage and Moss & Son Importers.

summer of 1858, Yates didn't miss a beat. He quickly lined his street with wooden shanties to house the gold-hungry hordes.

By 1860 he owned all the land between Langley and Wharf streets. His town lots sprouted handsome brick and stone buildings that brought in an equally handsome income. Just eleven years after he first stepped on these shores, he was arguably the richest man in town. It was a far cry from his humble beginnings here.

By 1864, the fort where he and his wife had spent their earliest days was just a memory. Governor Douglas was about to retire. The HBC post had become a city. Far from being the grand central thoroughfare envisaged by its builder,

Yates Street was now on the edge of a downtown core that boasted bawdy houses, brothels, and belligerent drunks. The population was waning. Victoria was in a state of decline.

But Yates had already left. In 1860 he had taken his wife and daughters back to Scotland, leaving James and Harry in Victoria with his sister Isabella. He returned to deal with business matters in 1862 and took his sons home to Edinburgh in 1864. The two boys later came back to Victoria, so our city's first innkeeper has many descendants here. Harriet Road reminds us of one of his daughters, and the six-lane downtown street still bears her father's name.

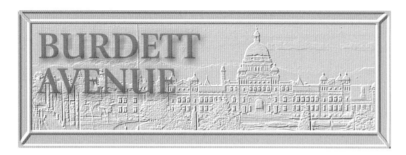

A great lady's gift of godliness

A few short blocks from where James Yates's wooden shanties provided places for gold miners to spend their money, a church made of iron helped save their souls. It stood on the east side of the main road out of town—a remarkable edifice donated by an equally remarkable woman. Her name was Angela Burdett-Coutts.

Born in 1814, Miss Burdett-Coutts had a privileged childhood, and at the age of 23 she inherited a fortune from her step-grandmother, the Duchess of St. Albans. She was a thoughtful, religious soul. Inspired, apparently, by her friendship with Charles Dickens, she pledged herself to helping the poor.

In the 1850s no fewer than four churches were consecrated in the poorest districts of London. Churches were built or restored in other parts of England. Bishoprics were established in South Africa and Australia. And in the Colony of Vancouver Island, an Anglican minister took the first step toward a relationship with a woman he would never meet.

By 1858 Reverend Edward Cridge was in his third year as the sole representative of the Church of England in Victoria. Holding services in the wooden church high on the hill above the fort and ministering to his scattered flock had kept him busy from the start. But lately he'd been spread even thinner than usual by the recent and unexpected arrival of gold miners bound for the Fraser River.

In the few minutes it took the *Commodore* to drop anchor on April 25, 1858, the population of the Hudson's Bay Company outpost had swelled from 200 to 450. By the end of July, 6000 people had swarmed into the settlement and thousands more would follow. Transient they might be, but the church on the hill just wasn't big enough to hold them all.

Even Governor Douglas's efforts at law and order had not been enough to put Cridge's mind at rest. These men were a different breed—desperate people, desperate for a chance to make their fortunes in gold. Their impact was

Angela Burdett-Coutts

Bishop George Hills (left), flamboyant churchman and friend of Lady Angela, carried out her wishes in Victoria. This included overseeing the assembly of the prefabricated Iron Church (right), which stood at the corner of Douglas and Fisgard streets (where the Bay store is today) for 42 years.

alarming. He feared for the future of the town. Putting pen to paper, he carefully outlined his concerns in a letter to the Colonial Church and School Society in London.

Cridge's cry for help was heard and answered more fully than he could possibly have anticipated. He had hoped for perhaps a missionary or two to help in the outlying areas. But when the Society showed his letter to Miss Angela Burdett-Coutts, she responded by providing not one but several clergymen and—to his amazement—a bishop.

Bishop George Hills was tall, energetic, and enthusiastic. He had Lady Angela's confidence—along, some say, with her affections—and before long her endowment of a bishopric was complemented by an amount earmarked for a new place of worship. Hills was delighted. He

Built in 1865 as an Anglican girls school, Angela College was named after its benefactress, Angela Burdett-Coutts.

knew exactly what he wanted—a prefabricated iron church. Other colonies already had them; Vancouver's Island should have one too.

The cast- and corrugated-iron structure was designed and assembled in London. Wooden beams would support the iron-plated walls and roof. Bishop Hills himself inspected the church before ordering it dismantled and shipped to Victoria. Then he travelled to the colony and awaited its arrival.

Hills was not much impressed with Victoria's uneven, muddy streets or with the generally ungodly behaviour of its population, but he was pleased with the attendance at Christ Church. He immediately set about raising money for a

site for the new church, which was on its way around Cape Horn aboard the *Athelstan*.

Hills found the perfect spot at the north end of town, on the northeast corner of Douglas and Fisgard streets. Trees were felled and a foundation was put in place. In a ceremony rivalling any held in the community so far, Governor Douglas laid the cornerstone. Construction continued through the summer, and by September 1860 it was consecrated. Thanks to Angela Burdett-Coutts, the iron church of St. John was a reality at last.

The Baroness's beneficence didn't end there. More clergymen swelled the ranks of those ministering to Victoria's outlying areas. Church

When it was built, distinctive red-brick Angela College stood in almost solitary splendour on present-day Burdett Avenue, near where it crosses Quadra Street, which runs across the centre of the photo.

bells, an organ, and furnishings were gratefully received. Two boatloads of marriageable young Englishwomen swelled the population, and a red-brick school named Angela College provided a place of education for the colonists' daughters.

But it was the iron church that drew the most attention, and it featured prominently in early Victorian photographs until it was demolished in 1913. By that time its benefactress was gone, but hardly forgotten.

In 1871 Queen Victoria had bestowed on Lady Angela the title of Baroness Burdett-Coutts of Highgate and Brookfield. She was a Freeman

of the City of London. In 1881, having remained single into her sixties, she shocked all who knew her by marrying a man 40 years her junior. They were together for 25 years until she died, aged 92, in 1906. She is buried in Westminster Abbey.

Angela Burdett-Coutts never visited our city, but her legacy lives on. The iron church may be gone, but Angela College and Burdett Avenue immortalize her name.

BEACON STREET

So where's the beacon?

What's a Beacon Street without a beacon? It's a street that leads to the place where beacons used to stand, high on a hill, where they could warn ships at sea away from the rocks that threatened to tear them apart.

Long before James Douglas chose Victoria as the site for a Hudson's Bay Company fort, the hill at the eastern end of Beacon Street had its place in the history of this area. The Native people called it Mee-a-can, or "belly," because from a certain angle it looked to their eyes like a fat man lying on his back. Mee-a-can was once the burying ground for two fortified Indian villages nearby. Evidence of prehistoric burial mounds found on the hill in the late 1800s confirmed it was the final resting place of an ancient race, wiped out many centuries ago by disease.

It is said that when James Douglas first stepped ashore here in 1842, he earmarked the

Queen Victoria's birthday was always an occasion for celebrations in Beacon Hill Park—even before it was officially a park! This one took place in 1862.

*This is one of many "race days" in Beacon Hill Park during the 1880s, seen
from the corner of Douglas and Niagara streets.*

hill and the land surrounding it for public use.
Colonial surveyor Joseph Pemberton labelled it
accordingly on his 1852 map. But it wasn't until
1859 that Douglas, now governor of Vancouver
Island, officially reserved the land for a public
park, under the control of the colonial
government. By that time it had already become
a favourite spot for lavish parties the governor
held for guests that he entertained at his fine
home near the park's northwestern corner.

A cricket ground was installed in 1862. Long
after Captain W.C. Grant had donated his
unused cricket set to the school at the fort and
returned to England in disgust, cricket and
rounders became basic fare at Beacon Hill.
Locals played against the crews of visiting ships.
In the mid-1860s the Victoria Cricket Club was
forced to put a fence around its pitch to protect
it from the pigs and cows that wandered over
from nearby farms.

In the late 1870s, fears of a Russian attack
spurred the installation of a powder magazine
at Goodacre Lake, along with guns at Finlayson
Point and farther east along Dallas Road. The
threat of war proved to be unfounded, and the
guns were later dismantled. Which explains why
two blocks south of Beacon Street without a
beacon, we find Battery Street without a battery.

In 1882, the Government of British
Columbia gave Beacon Hill Park to the City of
Victoria, in trust. Its 154 acres, later increased
by some 30 acres, continued to be a focal point
for fun and frolic and were the scene of some
very interesting activities. The park was a

Looking down over the inner part of the racetrack, where a cricket match is in progress, towards the scattered dwellings along Dallas Road and the Sooke Hills beyond.

favourite venue for horse racing, soccer, softball, baseball, and lawn bowling. The racing track followed today's Circle Drive, Dallas Road, and Douglas Street. During the Queen's Birthday celebrations, large purses were offered to the winners. Carriage roads provided access for buggies and two-wheeled gigs. Men in white flannels escorted ladies who wore long gowns and carried parasols to protect them from a too-warm sun. A bandshell drew Sunday concert-goers.

In 1858 the Fraser River gold rush was the catalyst for Victoria's growth, but in 1885 Victoria had a "gold rush" all its own. A man from California caused a great deal of excitement by announcing that he had struck gold in Beacon Hill Park. There were large quantities of gold-bearing quartz to be found, he said, in the cliffs fronting Dallas Road. A few prominent locals immediately took up a collection and paid the stranger to keep this news to himself so the

town would not be overrun with miners and the park desecrated. The stranger returned to California, a great deal richer than when he had arrived. The men who paid him off decided that a little digging of their own would not harm the park. But despite their energetic efforts, not a glimmer of gold was found. What had seemed like a golden opportunity turned out to be a joke, and the Californian had the last laugh.

A few years later, in 1889, Victoria ratepayers approved a loan for development of the park. There was a competition for "best plan." It was won by Scottish landscape architect James Blair. That same year, a group of citizens headed by Joseph Heywood, a local funeral home director, donated 2000 trees and shrubs gathered from as far away as California and Philadelphia. Blair constructed two artificial lakes—Fountain and Alderman (later renamed Goodacre). The first stately swans to sail under Goodacre Lake's stone

The stone bridge on Goodacre Lake is still a favourite subject for artists in Beacon Hill Park. One of the earlier renditions is this one by Victor Arnold Wolfenden from about 1899.

bridge came from Her Majesty's Swannery in Cookham-on-Thames, England, and in 1932 the two lakes were connected by a wandering stream.

In 1890 a small zoo housed deer, buffalo, wolves, and eagles, and in 1891 the first peacock arrived, soon to be followed by a peahen. Many years later a rare white bear, *Ursus Kermodei*, took up residence in a specially constructed bear pit, but the zoo never did achieve much public support. In the end Queenie, the park's faithful old Clydesdale workhorse, beloved by Victoria's children, was the only animal left.

In 1911 the twelve acres facing Heywood Avenue were ploughed and planted. Grass and trees graced the park's northeastern section. But an economic slump hit Victoria, and between 1914 and 1946 lack of funds prevented further improvements.

Balsam, cottonwood, exotic eucalyptus, palms, Douglas fir, and Garry oaks grace the hill.

Where once there was a yellow carpet of broom, grown from seeds planted by early settlers, there is a mix of wildflowers, rose gardens, and ornamental displays. Every spring, wild daffodils wave to passers-by. A little later, blankets of blue camas lilies cover the grassy slopes.

Looking from the east end of Beacon Street, it's easy to see why the Indians picked this spot. If you cross the soccer field and wander up the grassy slope toward the summit of the small, bare, belly-like hill, you'll find a lookout. Squint your eyes and you'll swear you can almost see the sailing ships that first discovered these shores, almost hear the cries of the sailors as they exclaimed in wonder at the sight of the clover-clad shoreline, almost feel the warmth of the sun on the bare backs of those long-ago residents of this very special place.

Beacon Hill Park: Free for all to enjoy, but still a priceless jewel in Victoria's crown.

First man to run the fort; first woman to own land

Not too far east of Beacon Hill Park, Ross Street connects Ross Bay and Gonzales Bay and marks the centre of a waterfront acreage that once belonged to the wife of Victoria's first man at the fort.

Born in Inverness-shire, Scotland, in 1794, Charles Ross was the third son of a nobleman. His older brother studied medicine. His middle brother entered the ministry. Charles chose the fur trade, signing on with the North West Company in 1818. Four years after he arrived at York Factory, after the Hudson's Bay and North West companies had merged, Ross was appointed clerk at Lac La Pluie (Rainy Lake), Ontario. It was here that he met the woman who would eventually ensure that his name lived on in Victoria's history.

Isabella Mainville was the daughter of a European man and an Ojibway woman. She and Charles Ross married "in the custom of the country" in 1822. Shortly afterwards they crossed the Rockies to New Caledonia, as northern B.C. was then called.

The Company believed in keeping its men

Isabella Ross

on the move, and Ross was transferred with monotonous regularity. He served at several posts east of the Rockies for sixteen years before returning to the Northwest Coast in 1838. The faithful Isabella was always at his side, ready to carry out the myriad duties of a fur-trader's wife. She entertained guests, acted as interpreter, kept an eye on trading activities in her husband's absence, and mothered their offspring, who eventually numbered five boys and four girls.

She was a brave soul too. Even HBC Governor George Simpson was impressed by the courage she displayed. He reported that Indian traders had once threatened her son, in her husband's absence, and that without hesitation or fear, Isabella had taken up a pike-pole and chased the rascals out of the fort.

But the hard, desolate life in small northern forts afforded little opportunity for youngsters to practise social skills. Ross fretted about the wildness of his children's behaviour and their lack of formal education. From Fort McLeod, where he'd been sent to relieve the ailing John Tod, he moved to

This view from Gonzales Hill, looking southwest over McNeill Bay towards Ross Bay and Clover Point, was taken in the 1890s.

Athabaska, then to Fort McLoughlin, which he found particularly dreary. Ross, who was melancholy at the best of times, became the victim of depression.

When Governor Simpson told him he was to be transferred once again—this time to oversee the building of a new post on Vancouver Island—Ross was delighted. Fort Victoria was much larger than the northern forts he had served at so far and was clearly destined for prominence in the Northwest. Anticipating receipt of his commission, he sent his three middle children to England. The younger ones would stay at home, and John, the eldest, would work with him at Fort Victoria.

Arriving at the new fort site in June 1843, Ross, Roderick Finlayson, and 40 men worked

hard to establish the new post. Seven months later Ross was able to report good progress with building and five acres of land cleared for farming. His hard work was beginning to pay off. Then he fell ill.

It wasn't the first time this particular ailment—some kind of bowel disorder—had struck him, but this attack was clearly the most severe so far. It started in early 1844 and worsened through the spring. He wrote to his friend Dr. Tolmie for medical advice but begged him not to prescribe his usual remedy, exercise, because "I have enough here."

Then, in June, came the crisis. After five days of terrible suffering, probably the result of a ruptured appendix, Ross succumbed. He was the first European to die at the fort and the first to

Charles Ross Jr., shown here with his family, was the third of the Rosses' nine children. He had clearly not forgotten his father's Scottish roots.

be buried in the small HBC graveyard amid pastureland at today's intersection of Douglas and Johnson streets.

Fifteen years later this graveyard was abandoned in favour of a new burying ground on the outskirts of town. Wandering pigs had rooted up too many corpses, and in any case, the old graveyard was impeding the progress of Victoria's growing, gold-rush-fuelled commercial activities. The decision was made to move the remains to a safer spot. Charles Ross's was just one of many coffins carried by a work-party of prisoners—a chain gang—to the Quadra Street Cemetery.

By this time, Isabella was well established on her own property. After Charles's death she had taken her younger children, including the three who had returned from England, to Washington Territory, where her two grown boys were farmers. But in the early 1850s she returned and purchased a 99-acre strip of land along the waterfront east of Clover Point. The property stretched up from Ross Bay, just west of today's Arnold Avenue, behind Fairfield Plaza to the top of Gonzales Hill, over to Harling Point, then west again along the waterfront. Here, on the western portion of her land, British Columbia's first registered female landowner built a home for herself and her children. She named her property Fowl Bay Farm in recognition of the abundant bird life thereabouts.

Isabella was in good company. To the west, between her property and Beacon Hill, was Governor James Douglas's Fairfield Farm. To the north was colonial surveyor Joseph Pemberton's huge Gonzales estate. To the east was *Beaver* captain William McNeill's property, which shared a boundary with land now owned by Charles's old friend John Tod.

Unfortunately, Fowl Bay Farm did not do well. Although Isabella's five daughters grew up

The upper painting by Georgina M. de L'Aubinire shows "Ross Bay District Prior to the Establishment of the Cemetery." By the 1920s (below) the cemetery was well established, though the trees and bushes that grace the area today were absent.

and eventually married, two of her sons continued their wild ways and were constantly in trouble because of their drunk and disorderly behaviour.

In the 1860s Isabella married again, but her union with Lucius O'Brien was not a happy one. They separated, and she re-assumed the name of Ross. Realizing that she could not handle the farm alone, she sold the farmhouse and the acreage to her son Alexander and lived with him and his family.

In 1994, Victoria's Old Cemeteries Society marked Isabella Ross's grave in Ross Bay Cemetery with this wooden headboard, based on a design that would have been common when she was buried.

When Alexander died suddenly, the family was left destitute, and more land was sold to individual buyers. A portion was bought by one Robert Burnaby, who sold it to the city in 1872; it eventually formed the original core of Ross Bay Cemetery.

Isabella was cared for in her old age by the Sisters of St. Ann. When she died in April 1885, at the age of 78, she had outlived her husband by more than 40 years. She was buried in an unmarked grave in the cemetery overlooking the bay that now carried her name. The location remained unrecognized until 1994, when the Old Cemeteries Society erected a wooden headboard to mark her presence among us.

Today a coffee shop stands on the spot where Charles Ross was first laid to rest, but thanks to Isabella, his family name lives on in Ross Street, Ross Bay, and the cemetery whose peaceful, park-like setting provides a final resting place for many of Victoria's pioneers.

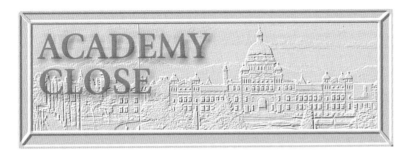

ACADEMY CLOSE

Pioneers in Catholic education

The Sisters of St. Ann cared for Isabella Ross in her old age, and they ministered to many other Victoria residents, young and old. Their mission was to educate children, nurse the sick, and wherever possible answer the needs of the people of this town. The Congregation of the Sisters of St. Ann was one of many flourishing communities of women religious in Quebec. Like other well-established orders, it was ready to take on the responsibility of a distant mission when Catholic Bishop Modeste Demers sought help with his diocese on the West Coast.

Demers had first visited the area in 1838, travelling by canoe and pack horse from Quebec with Hudson's Bay Company fur traders to Fort Vancouver on the Columbia River. The journey took more than six months. Visits to several inland forts in 1842 convinced Demers that the Bishop of Quebec had been correct—there was much work to be done amongst the Indians in this area and amongst the "wicked Christians" who appeared to have spread their vices.

Bishop Modeste Demers

Intent on establishing a mission that would answer the various needs of the small HBC-centred community, Demers returned to Quebec and visited the Sisters of St. Ann at St. Jacques. His invitation to take part in his newest venture on the West Coast was received with unqualified enthusiasm. All of the order's 45 sisters offered to help. Four were chosen.

By mid-April 1858, Sister Mary of the Sacred Heart, Sister Mary Lumena, Sister Mary of the Conception, and Sister Mary Angele were on their way. Following the route taken by so many others before them, the Sisters sailed from Montreal to New York and then on to Aspinwall, at the east end of the Isthmus of Panama. After a three-hour train journey they were in Panama City, boarding a steamer for San Francisco. Travelling via Portland and Bellingham, the women finally arrived at Victoria on June 5. Including a two-week stopover in San Francisco, the journey had taken them almost two months.

The Sisters were shocked and amazed at the vision that awaited them. They had expected a fort and a few houses. Instead there were streets filled with people, houses, and dozens of tents. The gold rush that had started a few weeks earlier was gathering momentum. Each steamer that arrived carried more men bound for the gold fields and the fortune they believed awaited them there.

Members of the local Catholic population hastened to greet the Sisters. The Helmckens hosted the new arrivals at dinner. Then as day turned to evening, they were escorted to their new home on what is now Humboldt Street. Marie Mainville, who had accompanied the Sisters from Quebec, helped them settle in. A local woman, Mrs. Reed, brought water and wood. Unpacking their few belongings, the Sisters rested until daybreak.

The next morning they took stock of their surroundings. "St. Ann's, Victoria," was a crude log cabin with broken windows and unlocked doors that had been built in 1845 by an HBC employee. Its six-metre by ten-metre cedar frame contained two rooms separated by a partition and a chimney.

With energy and fortitude the Sisters applied themselves to the task at hand. Classes started two days later, and they lived on one side of the

The original "St. Ann's, Victoria," was a small log cabin on Heywood Street near Humboldt.
In 1974 the building was moved to a location beside Helmcken House
and the Royal British Columbia Museum.

In 1871 the Sisters of St. Ann built a new academy on the grounds of their Humboldt Street property (above). By 1910 two new sections had been added, one on either side of the original four-storey building (below). In 1998 a restored St. Ann's housed government offices, and the chapel, sitting rooms, and grounds were open to the public.

SISTER MARY OF THE SACRED HEART | SISTER MARY ANGELE | SISTER MARY LUMENA | SISTER MARY OF THE CONCEPTION

The first four Sisters of St. Ann to arrive in Victoria prepared the way for a Catholic presence that made an important contribution to the city and the province

partition, taught on the other. This was not the first school. In the very early days, lessons had been provided in the fort, and in 1853 a school had been built out near Craigflower Farm. But education had been a somewhat haphazard affair. St. Ann's was the first school to have an official curriculum, strict rules regarding attendance, and a seemingly endless supply of pupils.

The first students were white, mixed race, and Native children—a total of twelve on the first school day. Within a year, 56 children had enrolled at the school, and the little log cabin with its board-on-packing-box seats was fairly bursting at the seams. Governor Douglas demonstrated his support of the new venture by sending his daughters to St. Ann's, though he later withdrew them, with regret, when the Sisters' insistence that girls not be allowed to attend formal dances clashed with his plans for them to accompany their parents to a ball.

In 1859 reinforcements arrived in the form of two more sisters from Quebec. One of them,

Sister Mary Providence, became the convent's Mother Superior. She was Irish-born and only 22 years old, but her education at schools in the British Isles, New York, and San Francisco had equipped her well.

Noting the overcrowded conditions of the log-cabin school, Sister Mary Providence rented a building on Broad Street. This was replaced in 1860 by a brick building on View Street, which housed both day-students and boarders. By this time it was a school for young ladies.

In 1863, eight more Sisters joined the convent. One, who had been ill since undertaking the long journey via Nicaragua, died in early 1864 and was buried in the convent's private graveyard on the grounds around the log cabin.

That same year the Sisters established a boarding school for Native girls in Quamichan, a 65-kilometre canoe trip from Victoria.

In 1871 a new four-storey school building arose on the Humboldt Street property. It was

This photo shows one of St. Ann's classrooms in about 1906.

known as St. Ann's Academy. In 1886 a new entrance and east wing (identical to the 1871 wing, now known as the west wing) enlarged the school. The chapel, originally a free-standing church on Humboldt, was moved in behind the Academy's new centre section. In 1910 the Hooper wing (designed by architect Thomas Hooper) was added at the west end. It held additional classrooms and an art studio, museum, auditorium, library, and dormitories.

Besides the work of education, the Sisters were involved in health care. St. Joseph's Hospital, opened in 1876, loomed on the north side of Humboldt Street.

By the early 1900s, St. Ann's, Victoria, was the central hub of activities that extended all over the province of British Columbia and into Alaska and the Yukon. Many of the first Sisters who served here had passed on, but thanks to the records in the Sisters of St. Ann Archives, we can follow their journey through life. A revered section at Ross Bay Cemetery reminds us of these remarkable women.

Between Humboldt Street and Academy Close, the convent that once stood almost alone nestles among modern buildings. And tucked away beside Helmcken House, close to the Royal British Columbia Museum, a simple log cabin stands as a mute reminder of the four Sisters who gave our pioneer children the first formal schooling they had ever known.

The Boston sailor who settled in Oak Bay

Today, McNeill Avenue dashes from west to east across the southern portion of Oak Bay. In the 1850s it marked the northern boundary of the parcel of land that lay east of Isabella Ross's farm—land belonging to the area's first American resident, William Henry McNeill.

McNeill was born in Boston in 1801. A Master Mariner at the age of twenty, he was in command of the brig *Llama* when he arrived on the West Coast in 1831. It wasn't his first foray to these shores—records tell us he explored this coast as early as 1824—but the Hudson's Bay Company would have been happier if it had been his last. Competition was neither desired nor welcomed, so when McNeill appeared on the horizon as an independent trader, the HBC harrumphed its disapproval.

Attempts to deter, dissuade, and demoralize the intruder were ignored, so a novel purchase agreement was proposed. The offer was too good to refuse. In 1832 McNeill sold the brig and its cargo to the HBC but

Captain William Henry McNeill

remained in command of the *Llama* and began a successful career with the Company that would span more than 30 years.

In 1837 McNeill became captain of the *Beaver*, newly arrived from England and the first steam paddlewheeler to ply the waters of the North Pacific. The *Beaver* was in a class of its own— the 101-foot vessel made of British oak, fir, and African teak was specifically designed to withstand the rigours of the journey around South America. Large greenheart timbers supported her furnaces, boilers, and 70 horsepower engines. A crew of 31 was required to sail her, and she consumed enormous quantities of wood. But she could negotiate the narrowest of channels and made a great impression on the Natives.

The *Beaver* made the long voyage around Cape Horn under sail, but was operating under steam by the time McNeill took command. He immediately explored the southern shores of Vancouver Island, and it was his favourable report on the area that inspired the HBC to consider it for a northern presence.

The SS Beaver *off Victoria in 1846. The fort is in the background.*
This painting is from the Hudson's Bay Collection.

In 1842 James Douglas confirmed that "Camosack" would serve the HBC well.

By the time Douglas and his working party arrived aboard the *Beaver* in 1843, Captain McNeill was ready to move on. Resigning his command, he visited England briefly, then returned in 1844 to find Fort Victoria up and running. He continued on to points north. Appointed chief factor in 1856, he was in charge of Fort Simpson and then commanded the steamship *Enterprise* before returning to a waterfront acreage next to Isabella Ross's property in 1863. The farmhouse on his 200-acre Shoal Bay property was a wonderful place

for his children and grandchildren. The only person missing was his first wife, Mathilda.

Mathilda was a Kaigani Haida chief, a successful trader in her own right who had helped her husband become the formidable force that so threatened the HBC. They married in 1830. Mathilda bore twelve children, ten of whom survived to adulthood. It was a haemorrhage following the birth of the last-born, twins, that resulted in Mathilda's demise at Fort Rupert in 1850.

Settling his family on his waterfront farm, McNeill brought a second wife, a high-ranking Nisga'a woman called Martha, to share his home.

The younger McNeills attended school at the fort along with the children of Charles Ross, James Douglas, John Work, and John Tod.

McNeill, American to the core, never became a British subject. His love for the sea kept him sailing well into his seventies. He eventually retired at 73 and died a year later, in 1875, at his home near Gonzales Point. Bishop Edward Cridge performed the funeral at the Reformed Episcopal Church, and the coffin was borne by such notables as Dr. W.F. Tolmie, Roderick Finlayson, and Sir James Douglas. He was buried at Ross Bay Cemetery.

McNeill's son and namesake took over the family farm. Unlike the other McNeill boys, William had done well and was a sea captain like his father. In 1853 he married Mary, daughter of Donald Macaulay of Viewfield Farm. (Macaulay had once served on the *Llama* with William McNeill Sr.) Mary's sister Flora married John Tod's son James, who farmed the top of Cedar Hill Road, and the Tods and McNeills remained close.

William Jr. died at age 57, the result of injuries suffered in a buggy accident a year earlier. Shortly afterwards a fire destroyed the McNeill farmhouse and with it the last evidence of William H. McNeill, first American to settle in south Oak Bay. He is remembered in Port McNeill, McNeill Avenue, and in McNeill Bay, where a welcoming lamp once hung in a farmhouse window and the toot of a ship's whistle told a family that father was on his way home.

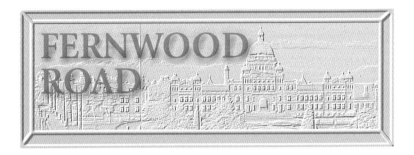

FERNWOOD ROAD

The Pearses called it home

A few feet west of Captain William McNeill's grave is the last resting place of the first person to be buried in Ross Bay Cemetery—Laetitia, wife of Benjamin William Pearse, the father of Fernwood.

Born in Devonshire, England, in 1832, Pearse was only nineteen years old when he left a lucrative position with the English government and set sail for Victoria aboard the *Norman Morison*. Hired to work for newly appointed governor James Douglas, he had been named assistant to his lifelong friend, surveyor-general Joseph D. Pemberton.

Starting in 1852 the two men conducted preliminary surveys of the Island's coastline, then worked on a plan to achieve settlement within the town of Victoria and encourage farming in the outer areas. By the time they had finished, the two friends knew southern Vancouver Island better than anyone. This knowledge would stand them in good stead.

As land surveyors, Pemberton and Pearse had first choice of desirable properties and, unlike many others, the money to pay for them. They decided to settle beyond the city's eastern boundary, just east of Cook Street. Pemberton bought a huge tract that included most of southern Oak Bay. In early 1857, just before the influx of gold seekers sent land prices skyrocketing upwards, Pearse put a downpayment on 190 acres of land directly north of his friend.

Pearse's land stretched from present-day Oak Bay Avenue—the boundary he shared with Pemberton—up to Bay Street, and from Fernwood Road to Foul Bay Road. He had chosen wisely. The HBC discounted rocks and swampland; Pearse's acreage, considered unsuitable for farming, only cost him 95 pounds. But money isn't everything, said his detractors. Why on earth would anyone want to move so far from civilization?

In those days, Fernwood was so far out of Victoria that it could be reached only by a trail that ran eastward from what is now Blanshard Street through the oak-studded countryside. Fort Street as far as Cook was a swampy wasteland, covered with alder and willow trees. Pemberton's 1860 survey described Fernwood as a mixture of swamp grass, clover, wildflowers, blossoming shrubs, and the ever-present rocks.

Rocks didn't bother Pearse one bit. In fact, he often relaxed by sitting on a stone outcropping that afforded a magnificent view of his investment, puffs of smoke from his favourite pipe wafting lazily on the breeze. One day, he told himself, I will make my home here.

"Fernwood," set in 300 acres that were purchased by Pearse in 1858, was built with stone from the land on which it stood and boasted panoramic views second to none.

And so he did. Using the same rock that had so often supported his weight, he built one of the first stone houses in B.C. It stood near the intersection of present-day Begbie and Vining streets. The house, and his estate, boasted one name: "Fernwood."

In 1864 Pearse succeeded Pemberton as surveyor-general of the Colony of Vancouver Island. He held a seat in the upper house and became a member of the executive council. In 1867, when Vancouver Island joined British Columbia, he continued in the service of the Crown, and after confederation with the Dominion of Canada, he became chief commissioner of Lands and Works. In 1871 he retired to enjoy his lovely home.

"Fernwood" sat surrounded by grand old oaks and firs, on a high point covered with honeysuckle, ivy, roses, and other beautiful flowers. Shrubs and rare plants abounded. Well-kept roads and paths wound through the parks and lawns. Moss-covered banks and ferny dells bordered the brook that bubbled its way through the grounds.

Beyond the formal gardens, the pastoral scene that greeted the eye rivalled any in Devonshire. Meadows, farms, gardens, and fields of gently waving grass stretched as far as the eye could see. To the east, the waters of Oak Bay sparkled in the sunshine. Beyond them, Mount Baker and Mount Rainier's peaks punctuated the skyline. To the south, the Olympic Mountains formed a majestic backdrop. And to the west, the still-small city of Victoria was framed by Vancouver Island's mountain ranges, silent and gloomy under their forest cloak.

It was to this idyllic place that Pearse had brought his bride in 1862. Mary Laetitia

Pemberton was a cousin of his friend Joseph Pemberton. Laetitia's future was full of promise. As they sailed from London together after their marriage, neither could have known that the fragile Laetitia was not long for this world. She suffered a decade-long illness before succumbing, suddenly, at "Fernwood" on Christmas Day 1872. Just 32 years old, she was buried at Ross Bay Cemetery three months before its official opening.

Three years later, Pearse married again. Sarah Jane, or Jennie, Palmer was the daughter of a solicitor in Great Yarmouth, England, and was 20 years younger than her husband. She was well educated and had been trained as a governess for titled British aristocracy. Arriving in Victoria in 1873 to visit an uncle, she met Pearse at a social function. Bishop Edward Cridge married them on June 8, 1876, in the newly established Reformed Episcopal Church. The wedding, as reported by the *Colonist* newspaper, was a sizzling society affair. The church was filled to overflowing with a large and fashionable congregation, principally ladies who had assembled to witness the nuptials. The bride wore white tarlatan with a satin basque.

With the arrival of its new hostess, "Fernwood" gained a new lease on life. Dinners, teas, and musical soirees became a regular feature, and Mr. and Mrs. Pearse were guests at every smart event in town. Jennie quickly became one of Victoria's most gracious hostesses. In 1882, when the Governor General of Canada and his wife, the Princess Louise, daughter of Queen Victoria, visited the city, Jennie was invited to meet them. Resplendent in pale blue

Henry and Sarah Crease and their children lived with Benjamin Pearse in "Fernwood" when they first moved to Victoria. This sketch by Sarah shows "View from our Bedroom Window at Fernwood."

satin trimmed with gold and blue brocade, exquisite old white lace, and flowers, the elegant Mrs. Pearse took her rightful place in what the *Colonist* described as "the most brilliant scene ever witnessed in the province."

The Pearses' marriage had been blessed with a daughter, Beatrice Mary Kate, born in March 1877, but the child was often unwell. Eventually a permanent invalid, she died suddenly at the age of 24. On June 19 of the following year, Benjamin Pearse died of cancer at the age of 70. Jennie was alone.

Her generous husband had left her well provided for, and the rest of his $270,000 estate was divided between old friends and institutions that included the Royal Jubilee Hospital, Friendly Help Society, Protestant Orphanage, the future University of Victoria, the Old Men's Home, and the Dr. Barnardo's Boys Homes in England. His attention to detail was evidenced by the request that certain of his books be given, after his wife's death, to the public

Benjamin and Jennie Pearse

library, "provided that they catalogue them and place them together, by themselves, and that they are handled only by people with clean hands."

Jennie lived on at Fernwood for another 52 years. Among the many changes during her lifetime was the abandonment of carriages in favour of automobiles. Unable to bear the thought of parting with her faithful carriage horses, she kept them until they grew old and fat, visiting every day to feed them tidbits. When she died in 1954, at age 100, the grand old carriage that she had so lovingly preserved was sold for $475.

Her home was bought by St. Margaret's School, but in 1969 it was demolished, and the once-magnificent estate is now a high-density residential development. Benjamin Pearse, father of Fernwood, ignored by street-namers, lies with his wives and his daughter in the cemetery at Ross Bay.

The "hanging judge" who didn't like hanging

egbie Street connects Shelbourne Street with Pandora Avenue by cutting diagonally through what used to be Benjamin Pearse's Fernwood estate. Yet over a century ago, the man this street is named for lived some distance southwest of it, on property that once formed part of James Douglas's Fairfield estate. And it was Douglas who had helped bring him to B.C. many years before.

The year was 1858 and Governor Douglas was worried. The Cariboo was filled with rough-and-ready Americans who seemed to make up their own rules as they went along, and Douglas was anxious to instill law and order. Douglas asked Britain for a judge. Britain sent Begbie.

Matthew Baillie Begbie was born into a military family in 1819. He received a degree from Cambridge in 1841 and decided to study law. He practised for some fourteen years with only a modicum of success and had actually never argued a criminal case, but when the new colony of British Columbia needed a judge, Begbie got the job. Boarding a Cunard liner at Liverpool, he sailed to New York, then Panama, made an overland crossing by rail, then sailed via San Francisco to Vancouver Island. He arrived at Esquimalt on November 15, 1858.

The 39-year-old barrister and the 55-year-old governor hit it off immediately. What Begbie might have lacked in experience, he made up for in stature, and the two manifested similar traits. Like his new boss, Begbie was tall, imposing, and had the same air of authority. The two also shared courage, physical stamina, a sense of adventure, and the firm belief that what they were doing was right.

Four days after Begbie arrived, he travelled to Fort Langley where, in a double ceremony, Douglas became first governor of the new colony and Begbie took the oath of office as judge.

He left for the gold fields almost immediately. He had been warned that the Californians understood a simple kind of law—one that allowed a man to be essentially a law unto himself unless challenged by other members of his community. Douglas charged the new judge with administering law as it was practised in the British Isles. It was a huge challenge but Begbie, he felt, was up to it. A few weeks later, as though to prove Douglas right, Begbie sealed his reputation for years to come in a situation known as "Ned McGowan's War."

As a law-breaker and as a magistrate in California, Ned McGowan had experienced both sides of the law without succeeding at either. Now he tried to meddle in a feud between

Judge Matthew Baillie Begbie and two gold commissioners,
Peter O'Reilly (left) and H.M. Ball, in 1859.

two Douglas-appointed magistrates and found himself facing the new judge for his pains.

It was a showdown of sorts. McGowan and his cohorts were armed; Begbie was not. His ammunition was his intellect, and he put it to good use. Delivering an address that left McGowan in no doubt as to the rights and wrongs of the situation, he inflicted the heaviest possible fine and had McGowan enter into a recognizance to keep the peace. Justice reigned supreme and would continue to do so in the

mining camps and shack towns of B.C. for as long as Begbie presided over them.

Aware of the unfairness that often arose around Native issues, Begbie acquired a working knowledge of Native languages and often took an interpreter along on his travels. He respected tribal traditions and supported the methods used by Natives to discipline their own.

His reputation as the "hanging judge," though awe-inspiring and impressive, was ill-deserved. Begbie made no bones about his dedication to law and order, but in fact he disliked murder trials and imposed only a few death sentences in his long and illustrious career. He was not, however, averse to flogging. His sentiments were: "If a man insists on behaving like a brute, after a fair warning, and won't quit the colony, treat him like a brute and flog him."

A man who used words like weapons to scold, belittle, and intimidate, he angrily berated juries who refused to convict murderers. He displayed courage in even the most daunting situations. Men were in awe of his strength and respected his straight-shooting style. Recognizing the fairness and consistency of his approach, they began to govern themselves accordingly and observe the laws of the land.

Begbie travelled the length and breadth of the province, dispensing justice with equal fervour from the saddle of his horse or the stump of a tree. His somewhat unorthodox methods incurred the wrath and scorn of other lawyers, but they didn't prevent him from carrying out the spirit of the law, which he carefully adapted to suit local conditions and customs. His diligence was rewarded in 1874, when Queen Victoria further honoured him with a knighthood.

In later years he spent more time in Victoria and involved himself in local affairs. A considerably more sedate figure than in the rough-and-ready Cariboo days, he presided over

An unknown man sits in front of Judge Begbie's cabin at Richfield, near Barkerville, in 1903. In 1865, Richfield was the centre of the gold fields, and Begbie held court here when he travelled to the area.

Judge Begbie played tennis on the courts behind his home, which was east of Cook Street between Collinson Street and Fairfield Road.

county court and often amused himself by allowing the plaintiff and the defendant almost to come to blows before insisting on order and announcing his judgment.

Begbie built a large home east of Cook Street between Collinson Street and Fairfield Road. Between his house and the Strait of Juan de Fuca, the swampy lands of Fairfield gave way to the trees of Beacon Hill Park, which he ruled should remain an area of unspoiled, natural beauty to be enjoyed by young and old alike, free of commercial ventures.

Always impeccably dressed and sporting a neat Vandyke beard, Begbie was, from the beginning, a familiar sight around town. He had been made first president of the Victoria Philharmonic Society in 1859 and was first president of the Union Club. Theatre Royal,

Victoria's first official theatre, was a converted Hudson's Bay Company storehouse, purchased by Begbie when the fort was dismantled.

His favourite pastimes were duck hunting in the Fairfield marshes and singing in the St. John's Church choir. A dedicated churchgoer, he joined Douglas and many other leading citizens in support of Dean Edward Cridge and helped pay the legal costs Cridge incurred by his battle with Bishop George Hills.

A confirmed bachelor (there were rumours of a disappointing love affair decades earlier in England), Begbie was always in demand for social occasions. A gallant air combined with a love of gossip, gardens, and good humour made him a firm favourite with the ladies. His tennis and badminton parties were legendary and his dinner parties were among the best in town.

Sir Matthew Baillie Begbie

So large was his presence and so long his tenure as a judge that it seemed impossible to imagine life without him. But cancer weakened the tall, gentle, white-haired fellow. His friends rallied round. The Pembertons, Pearses, Trutches, and O'Reillys were all at hand as he refused opiates and eventually asked for time alone to make his peace with God.

Begbie died on June 11, 1894, at the age of 75 and was buried a few blocks from his home, at Ross Bay Cemetery. He had requested a simple wooden cross. Instead, an imposing tombstone marked his grave. According to his wishes, it was inscribed only with his name, the dates of his birth and death, and the words "Lord be Merciful to Me a Sinner."

Matthew Baillie Begbie was instrumental in keeping Canada Canadian at a time when lawlessness would have left it open to other influences. He is commemorated by a mountain in the B.C. Interior, a statue in a niche to the right of the entrance to the Legislature Buildings (the niche on the left holds a statue of Captain George Vancouver), and a Victoria street that bears his name.

First lieutenant governor of B.C.

*J*ust around the corner from where Judge Begbie used to live is Trutch Street and the home of the man who was British Columbia's first lieutenant governor—Joseph William Trutch.

Trutch was born in 1826 in the West Indies, the older of two sons of William, an English solicitor practising in Jamaica, and Charlotte. Their union eventually produced three daughters, including one—Caroline—who would also have a place in the history of Victoria.

The senior Trutches returned to England in the mid-1830s, and their children were schooled there. Like his father, Joseph was an adventurer, always ready to explore new territory and eager to make his fortune. At 23, the siren song of California gold lured him to San Francisco and his first experience with Americans.

Trutch was not impressed. His staid, respectable upbringing had not prepared him for these people, and they were equally unprepared for him. As far as the Americans were concerned, Trutch was stuffy, pompous, and arrogant. As far as he was concerned, Americans were rude, vulgar, and not to be trusted. That didn't stop him entering into lucrative business deals with them, but it did inspire him to move north after only four months, to what he considered to be a more civilized environment.

Oregon, he felt, was a great improvement over San Francisco. Much of the countryside was still unspoiled, there was good civil engineering work to be had, and best of all, there was a flourishing social scene. Trutch thrived in his new environment. His brother John joined him from England, and the two worked together on projects for John Bowser Preston, surveyor-general in Oregon Territory. It was through Preston that Joseph met his future bride.

Julia Hyde, an American by birth, was everything Joseph wanted in a woman—well educated, well bred, well read. She was intelligent and curious but, like Joseph, had no interest whatsoever in braving new frontiers without life's little luxuries. They married in Oregon City in 1855. Moving to Michigan soon afterward, they returned to the West Coast in 1859 so that Trutch could complete a surveying contract for Governor James Douglas in Victoria. One government contract led to another. Over the ensuing years Trutch worked on the Harrison-Lillooet road and the Cariboo Wagon Road. He and his brother built the Alexandra Suspension Bridge across the Fraser River at Spuzzum. It was the first of its kind on this continent.

The Trutches and a few of the O'Reillys on the steps of Fairfield House. From left to right: Joseph Trutch, Caroline O'Reilly (holding Kathleen), Julia Trutch (standing), Charlotte Trutch (seated), Frank O'Reilly, and John Trutch (on steps).

Along the way, he amassed a sizeable fortune from his business interests. Leasing ten acres of James Douglas's Fairfield estate, he built a home for himself and Julia on the crest of a hill, facing west over the rapidly growing town of Victoria. Magnificent lawns and gardens surrounded Fairfield House, which was reached by a driveway running along the south side of Matthew Baillie Begbie's property.

The view was splendid. It was the perfect place to bring his widowed mother and his sister. Charlotte Trutch was in her 60s by this time. Caroline was a desirable young lady who, shortly after her arrival, met and married a dashing young gold commissioner by the name of Peter O'Reilly.

Trutch, meanwhile, had been elected to the legislative assembly in 1861. In 1864 he was offered the post of chief commissioner of Lands and Works. When he accepted the government appointment he was forced to dispose of most of his business holdings to avoid any conflict of interest. The appointment had other, far-reaching consequences. Everything in Trutch's upbringing had led him to believe that the British were superior to everyone else, and he continued to uphold this belief in his newly adopted home. Like many other early English colonists, he had little respect for Native people. In letters home to England he often referred to them in derogatory terms. As chief commissioner of Lands he made decisions in

Cary Castle was home of British Columbia's first six lieutenant governors. It was on the same site as present-day Government House, but the vice-regal residence went through two incarnations because fire destroyed the first and second houses. Below is the ballroom in the original Cary Castle, which burned in 1899.

connection with Indian land claims that would have repercussions long after he was gone.

Trutch's entry into politics coincided with the growing concern about British Columbia's future. There were three choices, it seemed: join Canadian Confederation, remain under British rule, or become annexed to the United States. Trutch could not tolerate the thought of annexation, so although he was at first opposed to confederation, he later became one of its most fervent supporters. He travelled frequently to Ottawa and so impressed Prime Minister Sir John A. Macdonald that when British Columbia officially joined Canada in 1871, he was appointed the province's first lieutenant governor.

Travelling back to the West Coast by train from Ottawa, Joseph and Julia were met at San Francisco by HMS *Sparrowhawk*, dispatched from Esquimalt Naval Station. After a turbulent, ten-day passage, they arrived in Victoria and moved immediately into Government House, which was then called Cary Castle.

Trutch made his first public appearance shortly afterward. He laid the cornerstone of St. Ann's convent school, which today forms the central portion of St. Ann's Academy. Other dignitaries at this very special event included Sir James Douglas, Chief Justice Matthew Baillie Begbie, Mr. Justice Crease, and the Honourable David Cameron (James Douglas's brother-in-law, and the first chief justice of Vancouver Island).

At Cary Castle, Julia was the perfect hostess, arranging social events that delighted the local gentry. Among the most memorable was the Queen's Birthday celebration in 1872, when 400 elegantly dressed guests danced in the beautifully decorated ballroom, dined at midnight, and dallied until dawn broke the morning sky.

Sir Joseph William Trutch

For a few years the Trutches enjoyed their elevated social status. However, the old country and old country ways never lost their lure. In 1876, after serving his term, Trutch took his wife back across the Atlantic, and the two proceeded to divide their time between Fairfield House, England, and other parts of the world.

In 1880, another foray into government work as B.C.'s confidential adviser to the Dominion government saw Trutch involved with his pet project—the transcontinental railway. It would keep him busy until his retirement in 1888, at which time the Trutches returned to England. The following year he was knighted by Queen Victoria.

A croquet party at Fairfield House, the Trutch residence, about 1870. The house was built on land purchased from James Douglas's Fairfield estate.

In the early 1890s, Julia became ill. What was first supposed to be simple indigestion turned into a lingering malady that defied the best efforts of her doctors. In 1895 it became clear that her health was declining rapidly, and she insisted on returning to Victoria. She died shortly afterward and was buried in Ross Bay Cemetery. There had been no children. Trutch, alone for the first time in 40 years and unable to bear Fairfield House without his beloved wife, went back to England. He died at his home in Taunton, Somerset, and was buried there in 1904.

The subdivision of Trutch's estate in 1906 coincided with the development of Fairfield, although for another decade the area would mostly comprise small farms and rolling meadows. Eventually the long driveway leading to the Trutch home became Collinson Street, and Trutch Street was put through to connect Richardson Street and Fairfield Road. Now Fairfield is a thriving residential community. Fairfield House, long since renamed and divided into apartments, still stands at 601 Trutch Street, one of a small handful of private homes that are a legacy of Victoria's early arrivals.

Home of the O'Reillys

This short north-south street doesn't seem particularly pleasant these days, but once upon a time Pleasant Street boasted several beautiful homes. Best known of these—and the only one still standing—is Point Ellice House, the home of Peter O'Reilly and Joseph Trutch's sister, Caroline.

Point Ellice House was at the opposite end of town from Fairfield House, where the Trutches held their croquet parties and entertained Victoria's elite. It was at one such gathering that Caroline was first introduced to the tall, handsome fellow who would soon become her husband.

Peter O'Reilly was an Irishman, born in County Meath in 1828. His well-to-do parents were staunch Catholics, but young Peter forsook Roman Catholicism in favour of the Church of England and left Ireland to become a gold commissioner in Victoria in 1859. James Douglas, noting O'Reilly's years of service with the Irish Revenue Police, quickly appointed him justice of the peace and stipendiary magistrate on the mainland.

Peter O'Reilly

O'Reilly's journeys around the province included visits to Victoria and frequent invitations to dinner at Fairfield House. Caroline Trutch had arrived in Victoria with her widowed mother only a short while earlier. O'Reilly was in luck—the beautiful, intelligent, talented, and well-travelled Caroline was still a spinster when her brother introduced them. Their marriage in December 1863 was a splendid affair. As a beautifully decorated carriage arrived at Christ Church Cathedral, all eyes were on a picture-perfect Caroline wearing white silk brocade.

A few months later, O'Reilly returned to his duties on the mainland. Caroline joined him and they settled in New Westminster, where their friends included Attorney General Henry Crease and his family. Life in the capital of the colony was good, and O'Reilly wasn't thrilled with the news that Victoria was to become the capital when the two colonies of British Columbia and Vancouver Island merged. But Caroline was pregnant with their second child. It seemed prudent to move back to the Island

Point Ellice House in the early 1880s, when the O'Reillys lived there. The house was built in 1861 and still stands today, open to the public for tours and as a museum with furnishings, artifacts, and ghosts from the O'Reillys' time.

before the birth so that Caroline's mother could help with the young family.

At the end of 1867 they moved into a house that had been built some six years earlier on part of John Work's vast Hillside estate. It was a small house, and the O'Reillys soon outgrew it. As their second, third, and fourth children arrived, the home that was expanded to accommodate them resembled as nearly as possible the manor houses of O'Reilly's childhood. It was a huge place with full-length windows, high ceilings,

and a fireplace in every room. The drawing room, with its bay windows looking out across what is now Selkirk Water, was an elegant place to take tea. The porch was perfect for whiling away a summer's evening. A wide expanse of grass contained a croquet pitch—son Frank became a title-holder in provincial competitions—and a lawn tennis court that rivalled Judge Matthew Begbie's in Fairfield.

The entire family loved gardening. Rose-covered arches, flower-bordered walks, and fruit

The O'Reillys were an energetic, active family. Here Kathleen (foreground) sits with her brothers (in bowler hats) Frank and A.J. after a tennis match. Peter and Caroline O'Reilly are seated on the bench by the stairs. The other two men are navel officers.

trees complemented the huge kitchen garden that supplied almost all the family's vegetables. There were no live-in servants—family members tended the garden. When the children went to England to attend school, letters from home assured them their portion of the gardens was being looked after.

The O'Reillys were in good company on Pleasant Street, surrounded by prosperous families with large houses on waterfront properties like their own. Peter was often away on business in the Interior. Caroline travelled with him whenever she could. Like her husband, Caroline loved to be outside and adored horseback riding. When she was at home in Victoria, she and her mother spent many happy hours calling on family and friends. Her children led a privileged life, being prepared for adulthood with a good solid English education before returning to their friends in Victoria.

One child, Kathleen, was particularly well known and loved. She was a girl after Caroline's own heart, being musical and having a penchant, like her parents, for diary and letter writing. She was also a woman of considerable beauty, who attracted her fair share of eligible young male admirers. Most famous among Kathleen's suitors was a young naval officer stationed at Esquimalt, one of many invited to the O'Reilly home over the years. His name was Robert Scott. We don't know how ardently he pursued her, but we do know that their friendship endured even after he left Victoria and that their correspondence continued until Scott perished during a bid to be first to reach the South Pole.

Captain Henry Stanhope was another frequent visitor at Point Ellice House. He was apparently completely besotted by Kathleen. O'Reilly, it seems, was not pleased by Stanhope's somewhat dubious financial status, but it was Kathleen herself who brought the affair, such as it was, to an end. When Stanhope declared his affections just before leaving for England, she

managed to stall, hoping that he would go home and forget about her. However, when his letter to O'Reilly proved that the flame of desire burned just as brightly, Kathleen was forced to admit to her doting father that she didn't want to marry Stanhope and was more than happy to stay in Victoria with her family.

O'Reilly, meanwhile, went from strength to strength, becoming county court judge of Yale District and a member of the legislative council. He quit the bench in 1881 and was appointed Indian reserve commissioner. Faring for the most part as poorly as his brother-in-law in his sixteen years of Indian affairs, O'Reilly's commanding

Point Ellice Bridge, which spanned Selkirk Water close to Point Ellice House, was the scene of a terrible disaster in May 1896. The bridge collapsed under the weight of an overloaded streetcar filled with revellers bound for the Queen's birthday celebrations at Macaulay Point. Fifty-five people drowned. Some of the survivors were brought ashore as the foot of the O'Reilly's garden and wrapped in blankets from the house.

The grounds of Point Ellice House were ideal for afternoon tea,
while the gardens supplied flowers and vegetables for the table.

presence became a familiar sight to Native groups. They were determined in their efforts to secure land for themselves; he was equally determined that they should not have it without a struggle.

There were difficult times, too, for the O'Reillys. Seven-year-old Mary Augusta and Caroline's mother Charlotte died in the same year in the 1870s, and in 1885 Caroline and Peter's carriage overturned at the corner of Herald Street, leaving Peter with injuries that permanently destroyed his robust health. He recovered enough to continue his social activities, however, and special visitors to Point Ellice House in 1886 included Prime Minister Sir John A. Macdonald and his wife.

Nothing, it seemed, could change the O'Reillys' place at the centre of Victoria's social circle. But their charmed existence was slowly coming to an end. In the late 1880s, Caroline fell ill. All the money in the world couldn't help her, and even a trip to England for medical care proved fruitless. Poor Caroline died soon after the ship

Kathleen O'Reilly

landed at Liverpool; she was buried in southeast England. Peter was inconsolable. He returned to Victoria and spent the remaining years of his life with his children at Point Ellice House. He died at the age of 77 and was buried in Ross Bay Cemetery on September 6, 1905.

Nobody really knows why Kathleen stayed unmarried. She was never short of gentleman admirers, but it seemed she was not interested enough in any of them to take that extra step. She lived at Point Ellice House to the age of 78, long after Rock Bay had ceased to be a high-class neighbourhood and four decades after her father had died.

The O'Reilly family's letters, diaries, and other papers, now stored in the provincial archives, have added immensely to our knowledge of those early colonial days. And on gritty, industrial Pleasant Street, Point Ellice House is lovingly preserved as a B.C. Heritage Site, standing as an elegant reminder of the young family that called it home more than a century ago.

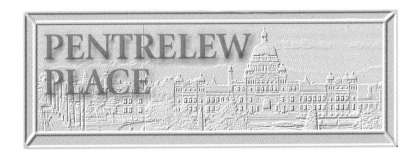

Home on a crest for the Creases

Henry Pering Pellew Crease

Some distance east of the O'Reillys, Henry and Sarah Crease built a home on the brow of Fort Street hill, where Pentrelew Place is today. The two families had been neighbours in New Westminster, and the two men had much in common: O'Reilly was a magistrate; Crease was a lawyer. He would later become British Columbia's first attorney general.

Henry Pering Pellew Crease's story begins in 1823, when he was born the son of a Royal Navy captain in Cornwall, southwest England. Raised in an upper-class environment, Henry wanted for nothing. He was educated at the best schools, and a fellow student at Mount Radford School, Joseph Trutch, would be his contemporary at another time, in another place.

One month after graduating in 1846, Crease began to study law. He was called to the bar in June 1849. That same year his family, their financial status in decline, moved to Canada West (later Ontario) to invest in the many canals being built there. Their efforts did not pay off. The senior Creases stayed in Canada for a few years, but Henry returned in 1850 to Britain and the woman he loved.

Sarah Lindley was the eldest daughter of a renowned botanist. She grew up in a large house on Acton Green, just outside London, surrounded by servants. Her days were filled with drawing, painting, and music. Like her new husband and his mother before him, Sarah was a talented artist. Little did she realize that this talent would one day give her a place in history as she recorded the growth of the city she came to call home.

Sarah confessed to Henry that she had first fallen in love with his drawings, seeing in them "a character which I was sure I could not help loving." The two were married at Acton Church in April 1853. During the next four years they had a son, who died in infancy, and three daughters—Mary, Susan, and Barbara.

In 1858, news of a gold rush in Western Canada brought Henry across the Atlantic once

more. Now 35 years old, he settled in Victoria, becoming the first barrister qualified to practise there. Encouraged by his earning potential on both the Island and the mainland, he sent for his family. They sailed on the *Athelstan* in the fall of 1859, arriving 163 days later, in February 1860. It was a joyful reunion. Henry had not seen his wife and daughters for two long years.

At first the Creases lived with Benjamin Pearse, still a bachelor at this time, in his recently built home, "Fernwood." Ever ready with her sketch pad to record her new environment, Sarah mailed the watercolours home. Her father entered them in the "British Columbia Department of Canada" section of the 1862 International Exhibition in Hyde Park, so that others who were curious about the new colony could enjoy them too.

In March 1860 Crease was elected to the legislative assembly as a member for Victoria District. In 1861, on his appointment as attorney general for the mainland colony of British Columbia, he resigned his seat in the house and, a year later, moved his family to New Westminster.

Their new home, Ince Cottage, was named after Ince Castle, where Henry had been born. It was designed by John Wright, who had also designed Fairfield House, the Victoria residence of Joseph and Julia Trutch, who were godparents to young Josephine Crease. Another son, Lindley, was also born.

The Creases painted and sketched their surroundings and their activities. At upper left, Sarah shows a scene on the deck of the Athelstan, *while Henry immortalized his first B.C. law office, with the notation "Barristering done here! Hooray for Crease!"*

Sarah Lindley Crease

The Creases were firm fixtures in a social circle that included the Trutches and the O'Reillys. Their financial future was secured through sound financial investments. It was a happy, profitable time, so understandably it was with some reluctance that the Creases returned to Vancouver Island in 1868, when Victoria became the capital of the combined colonies.

After the colonies combined, Crease remained attorney general. He travelled extensively between 1861 and 1870, drafting most of the laws of the colony. He was a member of the first legislative council, yet still found time for a flourishing private practice. In 1869 he was instrumental in forming the British Columbia Law Society, and in 1870 he was made Justice of the Supreme Court, a position he would hold for more than 25 years

Josephine Crease painted "Pentrelew," the Crease's Italianate villa on Fort Street hill, in the early 1900s.

Back in Victoria, two more sons were born. Henry died at fourteen months; Arthur survived. While the family was living near Beacon Hill, Crease bought a five-acre property on Cadboro Bay Road (later Fort Street) that boasted fields, oak trees, and a house ripe for remodelling. An addition was planned, but shortly before it was completed the house mysteriously caught fire and burned to the ground.

The following spring, Crease commissioned John Wright to build an Italianate villa on the site. In 1875 it was ready for occupancy. They named their home "Pentrelew," a Cornish word meaning "house on land sloping two ways." It was a perfect description of its lofty perch on the brow of what is now Fort Street hill. It was a fairly modest building, but more than adequate for Henry and Sarah's growing family.

While his wife established herself among Victoria's upper echelon as a renowned hostess, Crease continued to travel the province, holding court as he went. One family member or another would often accompany him on trips to B.C.'s Interior, and it was Lindley who in 1887 saw his father suffer horrible injuries in an accident. Henry's horse stumbled to its knees, driving the pommel of the Mexican saddle into his abdomen not once but twice. His internal injuries were so severe that he could not be moved for 48 hours, then had to be carried for 100 miles on a stretcher.

Miraculously, he survived to make many more journeys. On one of these trips, Sarah watched as her husband was threatened by a gun-toting wild man in the wilderness. Her reaction to these incidents was always cool, calm, and collected. Many potentially dangerous situations were thus averted, and both she and her husband lived to tell the tale.

Crease continued the political career he had started many years earlier, when he first campaigned for election to the House of Assembly. In those days, he had made enemies as well as friends. Notable—and most vociferous—among the former was Amor de Cosmos, editor of the *British Colonist* newspaper. De Cosmos, no fan of James Douglas or anyone else he considered linked to the Hudson's Bay Company, laid constant editorial siege to Crease and his colleagues.

Still, Crease prospered in his political activities. Although, like Trutch, he wasn't at first convinced that confederation was in the province's best interests, he helped draft British Columbia's Terms of Union with Canada. In 1896 his diligence was rewarded with a knighthood. The Honourable Sir Henry Crease was applauded in the *Colonist* by de Cosmos's successor, who described the honour as "a fitting closing of a useful and honorable career at the bar and upon the bench."

Crease enjoyed only nine years of retirement. He died at "Pentrelew" in 1905, at the age of 82, and was buried at Ross Bay Cemetery beside his daughter Barbara, who had died in 1883, and son Henry. Sarah, the wife with whom he had shared a long, loving relationship and who was a pioneer in women's organizations, outlived him by seventeen years, dying in 1922 at the age of 96.

Only two of the five Crease children married. The oldest daughter Mary became the wife of Frederick George Walker, an English lawyer like her father. Arthur, who as a child had been dandled on godfather James Douglas's knee, wed Helen, daughter of Judge Montague Tyrwhitt-Drake, a neighbour of Peter and Caroline O'Reilly's at Point Ellice.

Lindley, Josephine, and Susan remained single to the day they died. The Crease girls were all fine artists. Lindley and Arthur, who had been schooled in England, had long since followed their father into the legal profession, lending their name to a law firm that survives to this day. Arthur, last of the Crease children to survive, died in 1967.

Some 20 years earlier, "Pentrelew" had become a church. It was eventually demolished in 1984 and replaced, at 1201 Fort Street, by a newer church building. Only a garden shed, gateposts, and a few trees bear witness to the family that once lived there, but Sarah Crease's sketches provide winsome watercolour "snapshots" of the Victoria of long ago.

No writer's block for Higgins

*A*few blocks east of Pentrelew Place, a short street marks the southern aspect of land that once belonged to another creative individual. Sarah Crease and David Higgins traced Victoria's early days from different angles. She sketched her surroundings; he painted pictures with words.

David Williams Higgins was the son of a Manchester man who had immigrated to Nova Scotia in 1814. Higgins was born there in 1834. Two years later his parents moved the family to Brooklyn, New Jersey, where he received his education and appren- ticed as a printer. In 1852 the sixteen-year-old Higgins went to California. He became editor and part-owner of the *Morning Call* newspaper in 1856, selling his interest in 1858 when he got gold fever and headed north for British Columbia.

On its voyage from San Francisco, Higgins's

Mary Jane and David Higgins

ship carried some 1,200 souls, the latest of a wave of 20,000 gold seekers to journey north in search of fame and fortune. The *Sierra Nevada* was overloaded. Some fortunate passengers, like Higgins, shared staterooms; others, unable to find berths, lay on the decks or in the saloons. It was a particularly difficult, storm-tossed sailing. Most of the passengers were violently seasick. A few died and, in seagoing tradition, were consigned to a watery grave.

According to Higgins, three of the survivors formed an unusual relationship that would earn them a place in Victoria's history. He wrote the following story about them and included it in a book that was published almost five decades after these events were purported to have taken place. Higgins's cast of characters included George Sloane, a well-educated young Englishman who was fond of quoting Latin and Greek; John Liverpool, another Englishman, an adventurer and raconteur; and an attractive young lady known only as Miss Bradford.

Higgins tells how the unfortunate Miss Bradford was left an orphan when her mother died, five days out of San Francisco. Mrs. Bradford was buried at sea. Sloane, ever the English gentleman, took up a collection to help her establish herself in her new home. However, when he attempted to present it to her, Liverpool, who was also much attracted to Miss Bradford, became enraged. He knocked the money from Sloane's grasp and flung it over the ship's rail. A fistfight ensued. Both men were hurt, but Liverpool was definitely the worse for wear.

The next day the *Sierra Nevada* anchored at Esquimalt. Its passengers made the three-mile trek into Victoria and, like the hordes of hungry gold seekers before them, settled in the tent town that had sprung up around the fort. There, later the next evening, Sloane and Liverpool crossed paths again. Liverpool, who had with unseemly haste married Miss Bradford that very morning, was still smarting from his beating. When Sloane refused to accept Liverpool's challenge to take up a revolver and fight to the death, Liverpool spat full in his face. Goaded out of his usual good sense, Sloane agreed to a duel.

With their supporters and a large group of onlookers, the two walked to a grassy space just east of Victoria District Church, on the corner of today's Quadra Street and Burdett Avenue. In time-honoured tradition, they stood back to back. Liverpool, who had won choice of position, faced west. It was a smart choice. When they walked ten paces, turned, and fired, Sloane faced full into the setting sun. He fired and

missed. Liverpool's shot found its mark. Sloane, shot through the heart, dropped dead, the victim of Victoria's first duel. He was buried just a few yards away, in the Catholic section of the Quadra Street Burying Ground.

Indeed there was a duel, between two men with different names than those mentioned above. With his own, far more imaginative rendering of the events that took place, Higgins preserved the story, along with many other such interesting tales, for later eyes to read.

After this exciting beginning in his newly adopted home, Higgins travelled to Yale in search of gold. His descriptions of his adventures there and the people he came across have provided us with a rich source of information about those early gold rush days.

By 1860 the 24-year-old Higgins had tired of the gold fields. He returned to Victoria and met a fellow Nova Scotian who had already made his mark in this little town. Bill Smith, who had decided some years earlier to call himself Amor de Cosmos ("Lover of the Universe"), arrived in Victoria the same year as Higgins and took a great dislike to Governor James Douglas. Just before Christmas 1858, de Cosmos founded the *British Colonist*. Its sole purpose, it seemed, was to function as a vehicle for his unceasing, often vitriolic attacks on Douglas and all things allied to the Hudson's Bay Company.

Higgins became the *British Colonist's* reporter, making notes of his observations and interviews with townsfolk, then repairing to the paper's Wharf Street shed-cum-office to write his stories. It wasn't long, however, before the relationship soured between Higgins and his opinionated boss. Higgins left the *Colonist* and in 1862 started up the *Daily Chronicle* in direct

The second Colonist Building on Government Street suggested that the fourth estate was firmly entrenched in Victoria. Higgins operated from here until he sold what would become the Victoria Times Colonist *and entered provincial politics in 1886.*

competition. Neither newspaper did well. Higgins eventually combined them into what would become the *Victoria Times Colonist*.

In March 1863 Higgins married seventeen-year-old Mary Jane Pidwell, a Prince Edward Island native who had journeyed overland with her parents and arrived in Victoria several years earlier. The five Pidwell sisters were talented in vocal harmony. Ensemble singing was a novelty in Victoria at that time, and the Pidwell family home became a focus for social activity. Before long, four of the five sisters were married and had moved to California. Mary stayed.

David and Mary Higgins had six children. Oldest son W. Ralph, known as Will, was by all accounts a handsome and popular young fellow, an accomplished musician and singer and a "chip off the old block" who followed his father into journalism and onto the *Colonist*. Will married Edith Louise (known as Dolly), youngest daughter of Dr. and Mrs. J.S. Helmcken and thus a granddaughter of Sir James Douglas. Will and Edith rented a small cottage on Belleville Street, close to the Helmckens' house.

In 1885 Higgins built a large, Italianate home set at an angle on the corner of St. Charles Street and Cadboro Bay Road (now Fort Street). "Regents Park," set in several acres that stretched down St. Charles Street toward Rockland, was a fitting reflection of Higgins's stature in the community. Its two-and-a-half storeys featured vertical columns on the Fort Street side and wooden balustraded balconies above the verandah and bay windows. A dining room and drawing room dominated the main floor, while an exquisitely carved staircase led to the upper level's ten bedrooms.

Higgins was active in almost all aspects of the local business and political scene. He

Built in 1885, David Higgins's seventeen-room "Regents Park" was the scene of many social events. It still stands at the corner of Fort and St. Charles streets.

organized and became first president of the Victoria Fire Department. He was a member of the Board of Education from 1866 to 1869. A member of city council, he was returned to the provincial legislature as member for Victoria District in 1886. Three years later he became Speaker of the House, a position he held for nine years. As a businessman he promoted, and served on the board of directors of, Victoria's electric street railway system, which operated from 1889 to 1948.

Meanwhile, Mary Higgins too went from strength to strength. As Speaker of the assembly, her husband was at one point rendered almost speechless by Mary's involvement in the women's suffrage movement. Handed a list of 500 females in the Victoria area who were petitioning to secure the vote for women, Higgins was flabbergasted to find Mary's name at the top of the list. The petition was received, but it would be some years before women were given the right to vote.

Higgins retired in 1899. He died at "Regents Park" in 1917, at the age of 83, and is buried, beside Mary, in Ross Bay Cemetery. Lovingly restored, "Regents Park" stands today exactly where it was built, a stately and fitting reminder of the man whose colourful prose in books like *Mystic Spring* and *Passing of a Race* brought Victoria's early history to life.

Faces and places from B.C.'s past

While Sarah Crease and David Higgins recorded Victoria's history in paintings and prose, the Maynards' medium of choice was photography. Many shutters clicked as settlers and visitors captured the essence of the new city. But when it came to imagination, inventiveness, and style, nobody used a camera like Hannah Maynard.

Hannah Hatherley was an eighteen year old in Cornwall, England, when she married seaman and bootmaker Richard Maynard in 1852. They sailed for Canada shortly after. First son George, conceived on the journey, was born at Bowmanville, Canada West (now Ontario). Another son, Albert, and daughters Emma Jane and Zela rounded out the family during its Bowmanville years.

By the late 1850s Richard was restless. Life in Canada West was good, but not as good as the prospect of finding gold on the Fraser River. In 1859 he left his shoemaking business in Hannah's capable hands. Travelling down the east coast to Panama, then up the west coast to British territory, he followed the setting sun. There was money to be made on the Fraser, and Richard decided to move his family there.

Meanwhile, back in Bowmanville, Hannah had not been idle. Richard's letters, filled with descriptions of the scenes that met his eyes, inspired her to study professional photography. By the time he returned to Bowmanville, Hannah was ready to put her newly acquired skills to use in a new setting. Gathering up their

Hannah and Richard Maynard

Hannah and Richard Maynard first set up shop on Johnson at Douglas Street. Richard's shoe and leather business was on the main floor, while Hannah's studio was above. In the 1890s they moved a few blocks over to Pandora between Douglas and Blanshard.

four children and Hannah's photographic equipment, they retraced the route Richard had taken just three years earlier.

The Maynards arrived in Victoria in 1862, travelling on the same ship that had transported Higgins in 1858. The *Sierra Nevada* wasn't quite so crowded this time, but like the city at the end of its journey, it was fast falling into a state of disrepair. Disembarking safely, the family viewed its new surroundings with a mixture of dismay and delight. Victoria was still basically a tent town, inhabited mostly by miners. The miners, however, had money to burn. They wanted visual evidence of their new-found wealth, and the Maynards hastened to oblige.

Hannah and Richard set up shop on the dirt track that later became Johnson Street, her portrait studio situated above his main-floor shoe and leather business. Photography itself was only twenty years old, and the notion of a woman photographer was far too advanced for Victorian tastes. Nevertheless, Hannah's studio never lacked customers.

From time to time Richard still undertook prospecting trips to the Interior and northern B.C. Under Hannah's expert guidance he developed creditable photography skills and was soon recording visual images that provided the first real glimpses of frontier life and development. An 1868 journey to Barkerville with eleven-year-old Albert produced photographs of the Cariboo Wagon Road and settlements along the way. He was one of the first to picture Native scenes and would later receive acclaim for his photographs of landscapes and Indian villages.

Richard Maynard posed for his wife with a field camera and tripod. He learned the art of photography from Hannah, and his photos of the Cariboo gold rush are classics.

Although Hannah often accompanied and assisted Richard on his many trips, their styles were very different. While Richard's photographs were faithful recordings of places and events, Hannah's work was evolving into something far more imaginative and interesting. Richard preferred places; Hannah's primary focus was people.

Hannah surrounded herself with pictures of babies and young children. She would compose montages of miniatures—Gems, she called them—with hundreds of tiny faces carefully assembled into shapes that became more and more complex as each year went by. A copy of each Gem was sent to the parents of the children whose faces appeared in the montage. Originally intended as promotional items for Hannah's studio, these Gems took on a life of their own as new techniques were included in their creation.

Twenty years into her career, as she explored each new photographic technique, Hannah's work became increasingly more eccentric. After the death in 1883 of her beloved youngest daughter Lillian, who had been born in Victoria, followed by the deaths of daughter Emma Jane and daughter-in-law Adelaide, her work took a much more sombre turn. The Gems changed shape and form, reflecting Hannah's painful journey through the misery of mourning. Her "photosculptures" featured children in forced poses as symbolic spirit creatures, often standing on pedestals, draped and powdered to look like stone. Hannah called these figures "Living Statuary."

Later, as she embraced spiritualism, Hannah created double or multiple images that verged on the surreal or macabre. Often the subject of her own experiments, she produced photographs that contained four and five self-portraits, as brilliant as they were bizarre. One multiple image of a grandson whose parents had abandoned him, one through death, the other through alcoholism, bordered on the grotesque.

Hannah stopped producing Gems in 1895. Around 1897 she appears to have moderated her approach, reverting to her former technically correct but less creative style. Whatever devils had disturbed her seem to have loosened their grip on her life and her lens.

This example of Hannah Maynard's work with multiple exposure and montage features Hannah standing and sitting. Her nephew Maynard MacDonald is seated by Hannah at right and is also the statue on the pedestal.

Richard, who had continued his work in the field during Hannah's people-based preoccupation, died in 1907, at the age of 75. Oldest son George had worked in his father's shoemaking business but was now an auctioneer with a shop on Pandora Street. Second son Albert, who was called "the General," took over photography duties. Hannah eventually retired in 1912 and died in 1918 at the age of 84. She was buried beside Richard at Ross Bay Cemetery.

The Maynards' photographs, preserved in the provincial archives and reproduced for posterity in many history books, paint stark pictures of our province's pioneering past. The Maynard family name is remembered in Maynard Street and Maynard Park. But the front wall of 723 Pandora Street provides the most graphic reminder of the couple whose talents left us with tantalizing glimpses of the B.C. of days gone by.

CARR STREET

A life of sunshine and tumult

A year after the Maynards arrived in Victoria, a merchant returned to the west coast of North America from England. A street was once named after him, but he is remembered today as the father of a woman called Emily, whose talents as an artist and writer are recognized around the world.

Richard Carr hailed from Kent in England. Born in 1818 into a working-class family, he had no intentions of letting his humble beginnings dictate the rest of his days. He was an ambitious, curious adventurer who left home in 1837 to set sail for the New World.

Like Hannah Maynard, Carr took up photography, learning the daguerreotype process and setting up business in New Orleans. When it failed to show a profit he moved on to California, arriving there with fifteen dollars in his pocket on January 1, 1849—just in time for the gold rush.

A few years later, now established as a successful merchant in San Francisco, he met a young Englishwoman by the name of Emily Saunders. They set sail for England, married in Ensham, Oxfordshire, on January 18, 1855, and returned almost immediately to California. Richard was 37, Emily 18.

With the birth of Edith in 1856 and Clara one year later, Carr became a family man. By the end of the 1850s his future as a merchant was secure, but he was tiring of the West Coast and, against the advice of all his friends, decided to return to the land of his birth.

It was a huge mistake. Less than a month after landing in England in July 1861, Carr concluded that his American friends were right:

Richard and Emily Carr

Richard and Emily Carr stand on the front porch of their house in 1869.
Richard is holding Lizzie, while Edith and Clara stand at right.

he had been away too long. He confided in his diary, "I used to think there was nothing like England and the English, but I now find they are not exactly as I thought they were. They have their defects as well as other nations." But he was generous enough to acknowledge: "The change is with me…25 years absence makes things appear different even in one's native country."

Later that same year there was another, more devastating disappointment. A longed-for son, born on December 11, died after only four days. Little William's demise was the final nudge Carr needed. Convinced that his family would have brighter prospects in a newly settled, preferably British country, he determined to go west once more.

Sailing into Esquimalt on July 5, 1863, Carr noted that Victoria was a "beautifully located" town whose 6000-odd inhabitants enjoyed good sidewalks, well-supplied shops, fine brick and stone buildings, several churches, and three daily papers. He purchased four acres in James Bay and built a house on one of them. Near the house was a simple country road (named Carr Street in the 1880s, when Carr donated a strip of land to help widen it, and now part of Government Street).

On April 1, 1864, the Carrs moved into their new home. Constructed of fir, with California redwood trim, it contained every modern convenience, including a pump that brought water directly into the kitchen from a spring at the rear of the house.

In the midst of the James Bay wilderness, Carr created a corner of the world that was uniquely his own. He preserved as many trees as he could and cleared the land between them for orchards and meadows. He built sheds for his cows, grew vegetables, and planted several different kinds of fruit trees, bushes, and vines. His strawberries were legendary; according to one newspaper account they were so big they had to be eaten with a knife and fork.

Carr enclosed his little empire with fences to keep his cows from wandering and his children in check. There were six of them now, five girls and a boy.

Emily was born December 13, 1871. She was expected on December 12, but she later wrote, "Contrary from the start, I kept the family in suspense" until three the next morning in the middle of a snowstorm, when her father had to plough through the flurries on foot to fetch a midwife. It was not an easy birth, and it would not be an easy life.

Emily was a bright, curious, perceptive child with a passion for lilies and lilting prose. The flowers and animals and birds that surrounded her home were a constant delight, and the creatures in the cow yard were friends who, unlike her sisters, seemed to enjoy her loud, lusty singing.

Emily's world revolved around her strict, Victorian father and her quiet, loving mother. Richard Carr often took his youngest daughter with him on his morning journey into town. Hand in hand, they followed the planked sidewalk and farm lanes as far as Birdcage Walk (now part of Government Street). Then Father would stoop to kiss her goodbye before crossing the James Bay bridge to his Wharf Street store.

By Emily's sixteenth birthday, however, she was an orphan. Her mother, in poor health for

Emily Carr (lower right) at age 16 or 17 and her sisters (clockwise from Emily) Alice, Lizzie, Edith, and Clara.

some years, died in 1884. Her father, crushed and in poor health himself, died two years later.

Emily decided to pursue a career in art. She studied in California, London, and France, struggling to achieve recognition and acceptance as an artist. Over the years she journeyed into the wilderness of Vancouver Island and the Queen Charlottes, living and painting in log cabins, tents, toolsheds, lighthouses, and eventually a dilapidated old caravan that she called "The Elephant."

But the recognition she longed for proved elusive. She tried to support herself, first as an art teacher, then as a boarding-house owner. In 1913 she built a house on Simcoe Street, just around the corner from the family home, that stands there to this day. She called it "The House of All Sorts," a reference to the assortment of tenants that came and went over more than twenty years. Intended as a source of revenue, it

In 1918, Emily's Simcoe Street boarding house—which she later called "The House of All Sorts"—provided welcome space for her menagerie of animals, including (foreground) English bobtail sheepdogs Prince Pumkin, Lady Loo, and Young Jimmy.

proved a miserable experience that stalled her painting career for more than a decade. "I was not cut out for a landlady," she would later confess.

A turning point in the late 1920s was a trip to Eastern Canada to attend a display of her work at the National Gallery and to meet the Group of Seven—artists famous for their depiction of Canadian landscapes. "These men are very interesting and big and inspiring," she said, vowing she would "have my share, put in a little spoke for the West, one woman holding up my end."

Although inspired to paint better than she had ever done before, she was betrayed by her own body as she moved into her sixth decade.

The bright child who had become the striking young lady with the strong, thoughtful face was now a rather frumpy, grumpy woman plagued by a liver disorder, heart problems, and deafness.

Looking for another source of income, she turned to writing. *Klee Wyck*, the account of her adventures on the West Coast, was an instant success and won a Governor General's award. Then came the whimsical *Book of Small*, her impressions of life as a child. Other books followed, their vivid, imaginative prose painting word-pictures of Emily's life and experiences in the Victoria of days gone by.

Eventually, as World War Two neared its end, so too did Emily's life. When she died in

Emily Carr camping at Esquimalt Lagoon in May of 1936.

March 1945 in a nursing home (now the James Bay Inn) less than a block from where she was born, fewer than 50 people attended her funeral. She was buried with her family at Ross Bay, never knowing how much joy her paintings and books would bring to future generations, or that the house her father built would serve as a reminder of her time on this earth.

Subdivided many times, Emily's childhood world has been reduced to the size of a large city lot. But the family home, lovingly restored, still holds memories of a simpler, happier time. It invites you to stand awhile. Close your eyes and listen carefully. Out there in the cow yard, can you hear chickens scratching, ducks quacking, and the childish treble of a small girl serenading the family cow?

In her 60s, Emily looked back on a life of "Sunshine and Tumult," the title of the painting behind her.

BIBLIOGRAPHY

Source material at the British Columbia Archives and Record Service, City of Victoria Archives, Saanich Municipal Archives, Esquimalt Municipal Archives, Sooke Region Museum, and the Greater Victoria Public Library was supplemented with information from the following books and from James K. Nesbitt's "Old Homes and Families" columns that ran in the *Victoria Colonist*, Brad Morrison's articles on early Saanich pioneers that ran in the *Sidney Beachcomber*, various *Times Colonist* "Islander" articles (available in City of Victoria Archives and B.C. Archives and Record Service clippings files), and other articles by Ainslie Helmcken, Cecil Clark, John Adams, and Valerie Green.

ଔ ଃ ଔ ଃ

Adams, John. *Historic Guide to Ross Bay Cemetery*. Victoria: Sono Nis Press, 1998.

Akrigg, G.P.V. and Helen B. Akrigg. *British Columbia Chronicle 1847-1871: Gold & colonists*. Vancouver: Discovery Press, 1977.

Barnes, Fred C. (ed.) *Only In Oak Bay: Oak Bay Municipality 1906-1981*. Victoria: The Corporation of the District of Oak Bay, 1981.

Baskerville, Peter A. *Beyond the Island: An illustrated history of Victoria*. Burlington, Ontario: Windsor Publications Ltd., 1986.

Bell, Betty. *The Fair Land: Saanich*. Victoria: Sono Nis Press, 1982.

Carr, Emily. *The Complete Writings of Emily Carr* (introduction by Doris Shadbolt). Vancouver: Douglas & McIntyre, 1993.

Castle, Geoffrey (ed.) *Saanich: An illustrated history*. Sidney, B.C.: Manning Press, 1989.

City of Victoria. *A Brief History of Beacon Hill Park 1882-1982*. Victoria: City of Victoria Parks Department, 1982.

Down, Edith E. *A Century of Service: A history of the Sisters of St. Ann and their contribution to education in British Columbia, the Yukon and Alaska* (second printing). Victoria: The Sisters of St. Ann, 1999.

Downs, Art (ed.) *Pioneer Days in British Columbia*, Vol. 2. Surrey, B.C.: Heritage House, 1975.

Duffus, Maureen. *A Most Unusual Colony*. Victoria: Desktop Publishing Ltd., 1996.

Duffus, Maureen (ed.) *Craigflower Country: A history of View Royal 1850-1950*. Victoria: Desktop Publishing Ltd., 1993.

Duffus, Maureen (ed.) *Beyond The Blue Bridge: Stories from Esquimalt, history and reminiscences compiled by The Esquimalt Silver Threads Writers Group*. Victoria: Desktop Publishing Ltd., 1990.

Ellis, John, with Charles Lillard. *The Fernwood Files*. Victoria: Orca Book Publishers, 1989.

Fawcett, Edgar. *Some Reminiscences of Old Victoria*. Toronto: William Briggs, 1912.

Grant, Peter. *Victoria: A history in photographs*.

Canmore, Alberta: Altitude Publishing Canada Ltd., 1995.

Green, Valerie. *Above Stairs: Social life in upper class Victoria 1843-1918*. Victoria: Sono Nis Press, 1995.

Gregson, Harry. *A History of Victoria 1842-1970*. Victoria: The Victoria Observer Publishing Co. Ltd., 1970.

Helgesen, Marion I. (ed.) *Footprints: Pioneer Families of the Metchosin District*. Victoria: Metchosin School Museum Society, 1983.

Higgins, David Williams. *Tales of a Pioneer Journalist: From gold rush to Government Street in 19th century Victoria* , Art Downs (ed.). Surrey, B.C.: Heritage House, 1996.

Jupp, Ursula. *From Cordwood to Campus in Gordon Head 1852-1959*. Victoria: Ursula Jupp, 1975.

Kluckner, Michael. *Victoria: The Way It Was*. North Vancouver: Whitecap Books, 1986.

Lugrin, N. de Bertrand. *The Pioneer Women of Vancouver Island 1843-1866*. J. Hosie (ed.). Victoria: The Women's Canadian Club, 1928.

Ormsby, Margaret A. *British Columbia: A history*. Toronto: Macmillan Company of Canada Ltd., 1958.

Pethick, Derek. *Victoria: The Fort*. Vancouver: Mitchell Press, 1968.

Reksten, Terry. *More English Than The English: A very social history of Victoria*. Victoria: Orca Book Publishers, 1986.

Robinson, Leigh Burpee. *Esquimalt: "Place of Shoaling Waters."* Victoria: Quality Press, 1947.

Robinson, Sherri K. *Esquimalt Streets and Roads: A history*. Victoria: Sherri K. Robinson, 1995.

Stranix, Dorothy. *Notes and Quotes: A brief historical record of Colwood, Langford, Metchosin, Happy Valley-Glen Lake*. Victoria: Joint Centennial Committee, n.d.

Underhill, Stuart. *The Iron Church 1860-1985*. Victoria: Braemar Books Ltd., 1984.

Walbran, John T. *British Columbia Coast Names 1592-1906: Their origin and history*. North Vancouver: J. J. Douglas Ltd., 1971.

Ward, Robin. *Echoes of Empire: Victoria & its remarkable buildings*. Madeira Park, B.C.: Harbour Publishing, 1996.

INDEX

PHOTO CREDITS

B.C. Archives and Records Service

A-03407 (p. 8), B-09617 (p. 8), PDP02625 (p. 10), A-00903 (p. 12), B-06670 (p. 14), A-02914 (p. 16), A-01230 (p. 18), A-01260 (p. 19), PDP02892 (p. 23), A-02997 (p. 25), PDP 00286 (p. 28), A-01112 (p. 28), I-50645 (p. 30), E-00289 (p. 31), 1-29226 (p. 33), PDP 00034 (p. 34), E-01992 (p. 35), A-08840 (p. 36, t), A-08839 (p. 36,b), D-02128 (. 37, l), A-01483 (p. 37, r), B-06678 (p. 42), A-01910 (p. 44), A-07779 (p. 45), A-03422 (p. 46), D-09086 (p. 47, l), A-01826 (p. 47, r), A-01825 (p. 48, t), A-05578 (p. 48, b), D-01778 (p. 50), PDP 02246 (p. 52), A-04105 (p. 53), B-02262 (p. 54, t), A-03011 (p. 54, b), E-04394 (p. 57), PDP08516 (p. 58), G-09706 (p. 59, l), F-09874 (p. 59, r), PDP 00085 (p. 60, t), C-08601 (p. 60, b), B-00182 (p. 64), I-26551 (p. 65), G-01955 (p. 66), A-01441 (p. 68), A-01445 (p. 69), A-01447 (p. 70), G-04771 (p. 71), A-04720 (p. 72), PDP 05452 (p. 74), A-05961 (p. 75), B-01728 (p. 77), A-01302 (p. 78), E-02392 (p. 81), A-04386 (p. 82), C-09372 (p. 83), E-06994 (p. 85, t), B-01724 (p. 85, b), C-08992 (p. 91), D-08709 (p. 92), A-06621 (p. 95), F-02713 (p. 97), H-03148 (p. 98), C-09592 (p. 100), A-01185 (p. 103), PDP 00124 (p. 104), A-02555 (p. 106), A-06468 (p. 107, t), PDP 00250 (p. 107, b), A-02808 (p. 108, t) A-01266 (p. 108, b), B-06258 (p. 111, l), B-06263 (p. 111, r), D-00224 (p. 112), G-05357 (p. 113), F-08038 (p. 115), G-04990 (p. 119), G-04337 (p. 120), G-02724 (p. 121), A-03037 (p. 122), H-02671 (p. 123), B-00713 (p. 124), G-03832 (p. 125, l) A-02789 (p. 125, r), C-03857 (p. 126), A-03427 (p. 127, t), H-00981 (p. 127, b), A-02884 (p. 128), A-02883 (p. 129), A-02590 (p. 130), PDP 08967 (p. 131), F-01280 (p. 132), E-07617 (p. 133), F-05032 (p. 134), PDP 02148 (p. 135, t), G-01931 (p. 135, b), G-07048 (p. 137) C-05380 (p. 138), A-07737 (p. 139, t), A-07664 (p. 139, b), A-07803 (p. 141), A-01629 (p. 142), C-08746 (p. 146), PDP 04737 (p. 147), A-08339 (p. 148, t), A-08640 (p. 148, b), A-01102 (p. 150), D-03817 (p. 151), C-09042 (p. 152), E-07841 (P. 153), D-03510 (p. 155), A-02658 (p. 156, t), F-09901 (p. 156, b), A-08291 (p. 157), C-05218 (p. 158), A-01102 (p. 159), C-03921 (p. 160), I-51786 (p. 161), C-06135 (p. 162), H-06661 (p. 163, t), C-03924 (p. 163, b), C-03898 (p. 164), F-07698 (p. 165), PDP 02889 (p. 166, t), PDP 01394 (p. 166, b), A-01217 (p. 167), PDP03371 (p. 168), E-01370 (p. 170, l), E-01369 (p. 170, r), A-07820 (p. 172), E-01375 (p. 173), A-01507 (p. 174), C-08995 (p. 175), F-06336 (p. 176), F-05095 (p. 177), A-09184 (p. 178), C-03805 (p. 179), A-02037 (p. 180), C-05229 (p. 181), 65557 (p. 182, t), D-06009 (p. 183, b).

Other Credits

Canadian Illustrated News (p. 24, t, b)
Chris Gainor (p. 38, p. 136)
City of Victoria Archives PR252-7180 (p. 41)
HBC Archives, provincial archives of Manitoba P-407 N53A-231 (p. 6, b)
Heritage House Collection (p. 16,b, 40)
Hudson's Bay Collection (p. 143)
Illustrated British Columbia, 1884 (p. 13)
Metchosin School Museum Society (p. 32, 78, t, 79, 86, 87, 88)
Provincial Archives, Victoria (BCARS?)10616, #806 (p. 26, 27)
Public Archives of Canada C-4562 (p. 6, t)
Rodger Touchie (p. 14, b, 41, t)
Saanich Archives 1981-11-1 (p. 89), 1080-17-1(p. 116)
Saanich Pioneers' Society Archives, F285, #1 (p. 90), (p. 94), F559#29 (p. 99)
Sisters of St. Ann Archives (p. 140)
The Illustrated London News (p. 20-21)

THE AUTHOR

When she's not leading lantern tours as a volunteer for the Old Cemeteries Society, playing "Emily" at Carr House, or entertaining groups on guided walks around Victoria's historical areas and heritage neighbourhoods, Danda Humphreys is involved in acting, public speaking, research, writing, and editing. Her weekly column on the history of street names has appeared in the *Victoria Times Colonist* since October 1997.

This is Danda's first book about Victoria. She is currently researching the stories of more Victoria street names for a second book on the city's nineteenth-century pioneers.